THALIDOMIDE: THE LEGAL AFTERMATH

In memory of my parents
                    H.T.

To Ruth
                    C.R.M.

THALIDOMIDE
the legal aftermath

HARVEY TEFF, MA, LL.M, PhD
Of the Middle Temple, Barrister
Senior Lecturer in Law in the University of Durham

COLIN R. MUNRO, BA, LL.B.
Lecturer in Law in the University of Durham

SAXON HOUSE

Published by

SAXON HOUSE, Teakfield Limited
Westmead, Farnborough, Hants., England

Reprinted 1979

ISBN 0 566 00120 9

Printed in Great Britain by
Ilfadrove Limited, Barry, Glamorgan, S.Wales

Contents

Table of cases

Table of statutes

Acknowledgements

We are particularly indebted to John Miller of the University of Leeds and Phillip Capper, Fellow of Keble College, Oxford, for reading substantial parts of the text and making many valuable suggestions.

Our thanks are also due to our colleagues in the University of Durham Law Faculty for their helpful advice.

We are pleased to acknowledge the assistance given to us by the Library Staff of the Pharmaceutical Society of Great Britain and of the University of Durham.

The assistance we have derived from the interest shown in thalidomide by *The Sunday Times* will be apparent from the text. We would especially like to thank Phillip Knightley for information on several matters.

Our warmest thanks are due to Pat Gannie for her skilled typing of the manuscript and tireless help in the final stages of preparation. We are also grateful to the publishers for all their help.

July 1976

Introduction

Provision for resolving conflict by means of legal processes may justifiably be regarded as a hallmark of a civilised society. But essential as the right of resort to the courts clearly is, litigation frequently poses serious problems of expense and delay, particularly where the law itself is uncertain. Predictably, many would-be litigants resign themselves to whatever settlement of their claim is readily forthcoming, always assuming that they have had the temerity to put one forward at all.

Occasionally however an event occurs which makes such a dramatic impact that disquieting and perplexing features of the legal process demand an explanation. The thalidomide disaster is a classic example. Between 1959 and 1962 an estimated 10,000 deformed children were born in those countries where the drug was taken by women in the early stages of pregnancy. More than 400 were born in England and the final settlement of their claim was not reached until July 1973.

The particular facts of the dispute have never been and are now never likely to be fully litigated, but its repercussions and profound influence on the law are gradually emerging. A major consequence has been the tightening up of regulations governing the testing, advertising and production of drugs and medicines throughout the world. More recently, the sheer delay in meeting the claims of the parents and children has also highlighted certain technical shortcomings of our legal system, more particularly in the way in which it handles negligence cases and in the rules constituting the law of contempt.

Precisely because of its catastrophic dimensions, the thalidomide affair is proving to be a catalyst for changing the law in both of these spheres. It provoked extensive research by the Law Commission into the specific problem of liability for ante-natal injury, culminating in its *Report on Injuries to Unborn Children* (1974). The Congenital Disabilities (Civil Liability) Act 1976, based on the Law Commission's recommendations, has recently put beyond doubt the unborn child's right to sue for negligence.

Malformation of the foetus as a consequence of thalidomide was a very specialised instance of the much wider problem of injury caused by defective products. This whole subject is currently being investigated by the English and Scottish Law Commissions. At the same time, the Council of Europe and the Commission of the European Communities are actively engaged on similar research, which could eventually lead to changes in the present law of the United Kingdom.

In the long run, the most significant legal consequences of thalidomide are likely to come in the areas of compensation and contempt. It was a major influence on the creation, timing and terms of reference of the Royal Commission on Civil Liability and Compensation for Personal Injury (the Pearson Commission). Announcing the establishment of the Commission in 1972, the Prime Minister said:

> The Government have been considering proposals made from time to time in the past, which are now particularly relevant in the light of the Report of the Robens Committee on Safety and Health at Work and in connection with the recent concern over the thalidomide cases, that there should be an inquiry into the basis of civil liability in the United Kingdom for causing death or personal injury. It is the Government's view that a wide-ranging inquiry is required into the basis on which compensation should be recoverable.

The legitimate ambit of the law of contempt of court has been brought into the public eye as a result of press comment on the thalidomide case. The *Sunday Times* campaign amounted to an invitation to bring proceedings for contempt, and the higher courts were ·given the opportunity to mark out a boundary between free speech and fair trial. The Report of the Committee on Contempt of Court (the Phillimore Report) was delayed by the need to consider the decision of the House of Lords which banned the publication of a proposed *Sunday Times* article describing the testing and marketing of the drug. The ban was not lifted until June 1976, some three years later. An application contesting the validity of the House of Lords judgement was made the subject of proceedings before the European Commission of Human Rights at Strasbourg. Further changes may therefore be expected. In essence the problem is one of striking a balance between permitting free discussion of matters of public concern and safeguarding the authority and impartiality of the legal process.

In the absence of an exhaustive inquiry with full disclosure of relevant documents, it is idle to speculate on the precise allocation of legal and moral responsibility for the tragedy. A settlement has finally been reached (after some thirteen years) broadly in line with what the children would have been awarded on a full liability basis. Our purpose is not to apportion blame, but to examine the conditions necessary to establish liability and the legal principles which prevented inquiry into whether they in fact existed. We seek to examine the legal ramifications of a disaster which has managed to escape both the scrutiny of a full-scale public inquiry and a conclusive investigation in the courts, as well as to indicate the non-legal factors which helped to determine its outcome. In this way it may be possible to assess the adequacy of the English legal system to respond to such occurrences and consider how it might be modified to deal with them in the future.

1 The case history

It is a measure of the demand for sedative drugs that prescribed sleeping tablets alone are said to induce one night's sleep in ten in the United Kingdom. For many years among the most commonly used sedatives have been barbiturates of various kinds, but in recent times there has been a growing awareness of their dangers. Thousands of people are seriously dependent on them and overdoses, especially in combination with alcohol, are a major cause of accidental deaths and suicides. Understandably, pharmaceutical companies have devoted much time and money to the search for a sedative free from injurious side effects.

Thalidomide, a non-barbiturate hypnotic, was discovered in Germany in 1954. Preliminary animal experiments and clinical trials were conducted by the West German pharmaceutical company, Chemie Grünenthal, which initially marketed it in November 1956, as part of a combination drug (*Grippex*) to treat respiratory infections. Satisfied by clinical trials that it was a safe and effective sedative and hypnotic drug, in October 1957 they advertised it as a sedative under the trade name *Contergan*. Within months it was being distributed under a variety of names in numerous countries through the world, both as a sedative, and, in combination with substances like aspirin, to treat minor ailments such as colds, coughs and influenza. In Britain, where it was first marketed in April 1958, it was sold as *Distaval* and in compounds known as *Tensival, Asmaval, Valgis* and *Valgraine*. For two years it was available here over the counter, as well as on National Health prescription. [1] The American Pharmaceutical Association has compiled a list of thirty-seven such proprietary names, and even this is not exhaustive. In Germany it was sold over the counter without prescription.

In 1958 Chemie Grünenthal ran an intensive advertising campaign extolling the merits of thalidomide, with particular stress on its alleged lack of toxicity. In August the company circulated over 40,000 general practitioners in Germany with material on the drug, which included a covering letter promoting *Contergan* in the following terms:

> In pregnancy and during the lactation period, the female organism is under great strain. Sleeplessness, unrest and tension are constant complaints. The administration of a sedative and hypnotic that will hurt neither mother nor child is often necessary. [2]

It was explicitly stated that *Contergan* 'does not damage either mother or child'.

Similarly, as late as October 1961, only a few weeks before withdrawing the drug from the market, Distillers, who through their subsidiary Distillers Company (Biochemicals) Limited (DCBL) were the British manufacturers and licensees, issued an advertisement which said:

> Distaval can be given with complete safety to pregnant women and nursing mothers without adverse effect on mother or child.

Chemie Grünenthal's tests lasted for two years and Distillers conducted their own for a further six months. But neither they nor any other distributor tested thalidomide on pregnant animals.

Thalidomide and nerve damage

Early in 1959 Chemie Grünenthal were notified by doctors of various side effects of thalidomide such as disturbed balance, constipation, hangover and loss of memory; the company claimed that these were the results of overdosage and prolonged use. Many sedatives involve such side effects, which are not irreversible. More serious were the reports received from mid-1959 onwards that the drug was responsible for toxic polyneuritis – nerve damage signalled by a sensation of numbness (paraesthesia), followed in due course by severe muscular pains and cramps in the extremities, and disturbed reflexes and limb co-ordination (ataxia). These cases showed little or no improvement. In the worst instances partial paralysis occurred.

From early 1960 doctors in several parts of Great Britain were informing Distillers of such symptoms in patients who had taken thalidomide regularly for six months or more and there were numerous similar reports in Germany. But the sales promotion continued unabated, with advertising leaflets containing phrases such as 'non-toxic', 'completely harmless even for infants' and 'harmless even over a long period of use'. In April 1960, in an internal Chemie Grünenthal memorandum, Dr Mückter, who was responsible for developing thalidomide, stated:

> Unfortunately we are now receiving in increasing numbers reports on the side-effects of this drug, as well as letters from doctors and pharmacists who want to put Contergan on prescription. From our side everything must be done to avoid prescription enforcement, since already a substantial amount of our turnover comes from over-the-counter sales.

Indeed in May 1960 sales of thalidomide represented 46 per cent of Chemie Grünenthal's total turnover.

Though in general Chemie Grünenthal exercised extensive control over advertising by distributors, Distillers did mention in their promotional literature seven reports of adverse effects on the nervous system attributed to thalidomide, and in August and December 1960 circulated doctors with a letter which mentioned the risk of peripheral neuritis. Significantly, in January 1961 Chemie Grünenthal representatives criticised Distillers for this, pointing out that it might jeopardise the application for a licence in the United States: 'The open reference to polyneuritis in view of the worldwide importance of [thalidomide] is not at all to our taste'.

Reference to the nerve damage in the medical literature first appeared in a letter to the *British Medical Journal* (*BMJ*) on 31 December 1960 by Dr A. L. Florence, headed 'Is Thalidomide to Blame?' Two weeks later Dr Burley of Distillers wrote to the *BMJ* saying that due to the reports received the company had included in its literature a statement to the effect that peripheral neuritis could be a toxic hazard of the drug. Meanwhile several hundred suspected cases were being drawn to the attention of Chemie Grünenthal and in May 1961 six articles critical of the drug were published in German medical journals. In July the German company's legal department intimated that court cases might be expected and commented:

> Our arguments . . . would not be satisfactory in explaining why we made no changes in the package inserts . . . until September 1960. We shall be accused of contributory negligence in omitting to give any kind of warnings on the package insert, in case a patient has taken Contergan between May and September 1960 and has developed polyneuritis as a result.

On 28 July 1961, the company settled a claim out of court for DM750.

In the following month, after an article in *Der Spiegel* expressing concern, Chemie Grünenthal asked its licensees to drop the description 'non-toxic', though Dr Somers of Distillers felt able to say at a British Pharmaceutical conference in September 1961 that thalidomide, unlike barbiturates, was virtually free of toxicity. By this time, unknown to Distillers, nearly two and a half thousand cases had been reported to Chemie Grünenthal. The British company had itself received more than a hundred reports. On 30 September the *BMJ* published an article on the dangers of peripheral neuritis as well as a leader advocating greater caution

3

in the use of the drug, though not its total withdrawal:

> ... thalidomide ('distaval') has been tried out in Britain after its development and early use in Germany. It is a safe sedative and hypnotic drug and has the singular advantage of very low toxicity; many patients have recovered rapidly and completely after taking large doses in a suicidal attempt ... Now recent reports have described patients who developed a polyneuropathy after the regular use of this remedy ... while the incidence of this complication of treatment is not sufficient, in view of its other advantages, to suggest that the drug should never be prescribed, greater caution in its use is needed.

Subsequent issues of the *Journal* contained a number of letters associating thalidomide with peripheral neuritis. None the less, as late as 4 November there appeared a full page advertisement for *Distaval*, stressing its safety and ending with the words: 'There is no case on record in which even gross overdosage with distaval has had harmful results. Put your mind at rest. Depend on the safety of distaval.' In October 1961 it was still possible to buy thalidomide over the counter in seven German states, even though more than DM32,000 had been paid in settlement of fourteen cases.

However, within a matter of weeks, the mounting speculation that thalidomide was also responsible for the unprecedented outbreak of foetal deformity in West Germany (and elsewhere) was hardening into evidence too compelling to ignore. For this reason, Chemie Grünenthal and Distillers both withdrew thalidomide from the market on 27 November 1961.

Thalidomide and foetal deformity

It is evident now that in all the countries where thalidomide was taken by pregnant women, the number of deformed children born during the relevant period reached epidemic proportions. More than four hundred children were born with thalidomide-induced deformities in this country, and several thousand in Germany. There were others in Japan, Scandinavia, France, North America, Australia, New Zealand – in short, wherever the drug was distributed. Most estimates put the world total at about 10,000. The injuries covered a wide spectrum of limb deficiencies, ranging from virtual limblessness to relatively minor defects in a single limb, as well as defective sight and hearing. The main medical categories were *phocomelia*:

4

malformation of the extremities, or flipper limbs, such that arms could be very short and twisted and the hands, fingers and legs only vestigial; *microtia*: abnormal smallness of the ear; and *ectromelia*: absence of limbs or parts of limbs. The varied nature of the injuries has, as we shall see, led to difficulties in distinguishing the authentic thalidomide cases for compensation purposes.

Towards the end of 1959 there was a significant increase in the incidence of phocomelia and related deformities in West Germany. As Dr Helen Taussig, a leading authority on thalidomide injuries, has noted: 'There had been perhaps a dozen cases of phocomelia in 1959, whereas in the preceding decade there had been perhaps 15 in all of Western Germany'. [3] Evidence of the previous infrequency of the condition also appears from a Danish study in 1949, which found only one instance in a survey covering four million children. [4] In 1960 nearly every paediatric clinic in Germany experienced cases of phocomelia.

It was in September 1960 that Richardson-Merrell Inc. made its initial application to the American Food and Drug Administration (FDA) for a permit to sell thalidomide as *Kevadon* in the United States. How Dr Frances Kelsey, the medical officer assigned to review the application, resolutely resisted and ultimately thwarted the company's sustained efforts to obtain a licence is now well known. [5] The whole episode provides a revealing insight into the pressures involved in the process of drug marketing. What is less widely appreciated is the irony that in the United States, where a licence was refused, the chances of thalidomide families succeeding in a legal action against the manufacturers would have been significantly greater than in this country, as we shall see in chapter 5.

Initially Dr Kelsey had not been satisfied either with the information provided by the company or with its proposals for labelling. Her doubts were increased by Dr Florence's letter in the *BMJ* in December 1960, suggesting that prolonged use could result in peripheral neuritis, and by the growing number of clinical reports to the same effect. In May 1961 she asked the company for evidence that it was safe for pregnant women to take the drug, but she remained unconvinced by such data as were provided. It is interesting that as early as 5 December 1960 Richardson-Merrell had replied as follows to a doctor who had inquired whether thalidomide could affect the foetus: 'Unfortunately, I am unable to answer this question, since it has not been established whether or not there is any transfer of Kevadon across the placental barrier. However, we feel that, even if transfer does occur, it would be completely safe . . . '

In March 1961, Chemie Grünenthal, replying to a similar inquiry by the National Drug Company, a subdivision of Richardson-Merrell, stated: 'We have no experience regarding the question of Contergan and pregnancy ... we do not assume any influence on the foetus, judging from what we know of animal experiments'.

The withdrawal of the drug

Towards the end of 1961, as more deformed births came to light, several German doctors were researching into the cause. Speculation ranged as far afield as the belief that radio-active fallout was responsible. By early November, Dr Lenz, reputedly the first doctor to identify the association with deformity, was almost ready to rule out drugs as the explanation, when he was told by the mother of a deformed child that she had taken *Contergan* during pregnancy. On 16 November, Dr Lenz wrote to Chemie Grünenthal asking them to withdraw *Contergan*, but they were non-committal, hoping to satisfy the health authorities merely by inserting the words 'not to be taken during pregnancy' on the label.

At a meeting of paediatricians in Dusseldorf on 18 November Dr Lenz revealed his suspicions and on 26 November a newspaper article based on them brought the matter to the attention of the general public. Chemie Grünenthal wrote to the Drug Commission of the German Medical Association: 'Because press reports have undermined the basis of the scientific discussion, we have decided to withdraw Contergan from the market immediately.' Meanwhile in Australia Dr McBride, who had first notified the Distillers branch there of his own disquiet as early as June 1961, informed them in September of two further cases. On 27 November the Australian branch cabled DCBL in England, whose managing director wrote to the *BMJ*:

> ... reports have been received from two overseas sources possibly associating thalidomide with harmful effects on the foetus in early pregnancy. Although the evidence on which these reports are based is circumstantial and there have been no reports arising in Great Britain, either clinically or pharmacologically, we feel that we have no alternative but to withdraw the drug from the market immediately pending further investigation.

On 2 December Distillers withdrew *Distaval* from the market. Sjöström and Nilsson commented: 'In contrast to Chemie Grünenthal, which was only forced to withdraw the drug as a result of public opinion, the staff of Distillers showed quite a different attitude to the possible consequences to their consumers'. [6] This is evidenced by a reply Distillers gave to a doctor who inquired why they had withdrawn the drug:

> We took this action after receiving two reports, one from Australia and the other from Germany, that foetal deformity was thought to be associated with the administration of the drug in early pregnancy. These reports were passed on to us from commercial sources in the countries concerned and the data available to us is still incomplete. However, the type of deformity in the six cases from Australia and the eight from Germany follows the same pattern, in that they all involve limb deformities . . . It is still far from clear what other drugs were taken during the relevant period, but we felt that the coincidental report of such an effect was so serious that we had no alternative but to withdraw the drug immediately. [7]

Dr Mückter of Chemie Grünenthal, on the other hand, had been unwilling to let the drug be taken off the market even when informed by Distillers of Dr McBride's suspicions.

On 8 March 1962, Richardson-Merrell withdrew its application to sell the drug in the United States, but not before pre-marketing trials by 1,270 doctors ensured that over 20,000 patients, at least 200 of them pregnant, had taken it. There were in fact ten cases of thalidomide births officially admitted in America, and seven other cases of deformity where thalidomide may have been the cause. Thalidomide was still on sale in Canada in April 1962, according to *Maclean's Magazine*, and was used in Japan for a year after it had been withdrawn in most other countries. Over the years it has turned up from time to time in local campaigns for returning unused medicines. As recently as March 1976, thirty thalidomide tablets were discovered in one such campaign in West Sussex.

At the time when the drug was withdrawn the evidence of its adverse effects was strong but not conclusive. Concern was confined to the risks of the drug being taken during early pregnancy, and of polyneuritis in a minority of regular users. Several doctors expressed displeasure at its total withdrawal and Distillers left open the possibility that *Distaval* might be reintroduced for limited purposes, at least in hospitals, if this proved justifiable in the light of subsequent investigations. Early in 1962 the *Pharmaceutical Journal* drew attention to this point:

> It is hard to imagine a more difficult choice than that which faces a manufacturer who has to decide whether or not to withdraw a profitable drug from the market on the basis of evidence that on the one hand the drug may be dangerous to a small number of patients and, on the other, have valuable properties. So difficult must the

7

choice be that it is questionable whether the manufacturer should be the one to make it.[8]

But there were of course more urgent matters. Further analysis of the drug's effects was needed, as well as the collation of evidence from many different countries. If thalidomide were shown beyond doubt to be the cause of the deformities, who was really responsible? And who, which is not necessarily the same question, could be held legally liable? Most pressing of all was the need to prevent the drug being taken unwittingly by a woman in early pregnancy for whom it had earlier been prescribed, as likely as not in a container merely marked 'The Tablets'. Naturally help for the families already affected was imperative. In 1962 steps, albeit tentative ones, were taken in all these directions.

The first issue of *The Lancet* in January 1962 contained a letter from the managing director of DCBL which said that pharmacological studies and clinical inquiries were in hand. In the same issue, Dr Lenz expressed the view that the risk of malformation to infants whose mothers took *Contergan* between the fourth and eighth week of pregnancy was at least 20 per cent – substantially the same estimate as Dr McBride had made, though Dr Burley of Distillers put it at 2 per cent.

During 1962 reports of phocomelia came in from all over Britain. In most cases the mothers were known to have been prescribed thalidomide in early pregnancy. Several explanations are possible for those cases in which it was not positively identified as having been prescribed – incomplete records, fallible memories, or the patient's unwillingness to acknowledge the use of the drug through fear and guilt feelings. In a few cases, thalidomide might not have been the cause. However, in April Dr Somers reported to *The Lancet* that in laboratory experiments Distillers had produced thalidomide deformities in rabbits remarkably similar to those seen in man.

The Ministry of Health began trying to establish the dimensions of the problem in this country: the number of affected children and their geographical distribution, as well as what help was available from the National Health Service and voluntary agencies. The danger that the drug might still be taken by a pregnant woman was highlighted in a letter received by James Dance, MP, from one of his constituents, from which he quoted in a House of Commons debate on 14 May:

> ... I understood from an employee of the manufacturers that Distaval had been withdrawn merely because patients using this drug for long periods had developed slight peripheral neuritis. I still

possess a quantity of the tablets and would undoubtedly have used these again for insomnia in any future pregnancy.

The Ministry of Health then issued a warning to the public through the press and on 17 May the Chief Medical Officer circularised medical officers of health and general practitioners.

The concern felt in the medical world was reflected in conferences on thalidomide held at the Royal Society of Medicine and at the limb-fitting centre in Roehampton. Parents' associations were formed in London and Liverpool and on 16 July a *Panorama* television programme included a panel discussion on the topic. Pressure was building up for the Government to clarify its position.

The initial response of the Government to questions in Parliament was broadly speaking to defend the integrity of Chemie Grünenthal and Distillers and to emphasise that it bore no responsibility itself. Thus on 22 March Lord Newton said:

The drug was developed by German scientists and in this country by the Distillers Company and there is no doubt that the research and development teams consist of first class scientists. I am advised that the initial experimental work was done meticulously, and that the preliminary clinical trials were carried out by doctors who were wholly independent of the pharmaceutical firm which developed the drug.

Similarly Miss Pitt (Parliamentary Secretary to the Ministry of Health) stated on 14 May:

It ... is not the responsibility of the Minister of Health to tell the doctors which drugs they shall prescribe. It is the responsibility of the Minister to see that a service is available to patients. . . . the drug had extensive tests, in Germany first and then in this country. The side effects which showed later could not possibly have been foreseen.

But assertions of this could not dispel disquiet on the adequacy of the testing, nor allay fears that, in the absence of more stringent controls, there were undue risks of similar disasters in the future. Professor Graham Wilson, an eminent pharmacologist, maintained that more than half of the drugs issued in the previous year had been inadequately tested.

Consequently, on 24 July 1962, Maurice Edelman, MP, together with fourteen Opposition backbenchers, tabled a motion in the following terms:

> That the House calls on the Government to appoint a committee of inquiry to investigate the circumstances in which a proprietary drug known as thalidomide, designed to act as a sedative, produced over 500 foetal deformities during 1961 and 1962; and further calls upon the Government to appoint an independent statutory authority comparable with the Food and Drug Administration in the United States of America whose function it would be to supervise the clinical trials of new drugs and to authorise their marketing and prescription with a view to reducing the risk of similar tragedies occurring again.

The motion was defeated.

The Ministry of Health's defence of the way in which the drug had been tested was gradually becoming the 'conventional wisdom', and was reiterated in several newspapers and journals, notably in an article in *The Times* of 1 August 1962. *The Sunday Times* (on 27 June 1976) suggested that this version of events relied heavily on information received from Distillers. Certainly it was to exercise considerable influence on the legal advice which the parents were later to receive.

The initial settlement [9]

Neither Distillers nor the Government then were showing any signs of assuming responsibility voluntarily, and the chances of a public inquiry were becoming increasingly remote with the passing of time. State provision for the children was confined to such benefits as were available for the disabled generally under existing social security legislation, and charitable donations were not put on an organised footing until October 1962, when the Society for the Aid of Thalidomide Children launched an appeal for £500,000. It seemed that the only way in which the parents could have the whole matter thoroughly investigated, with at least some chance of adequate compensation, was by recourse to the courts. Pursuing a personal injuries claim through litigation is not the happiest of experiences at the best of times. It need hardly be stressed how much more intimidating and distressing such a prospect must have been for parents pitted against a powerful company with the financial resources to withstand an unsuccessful outcome, while needing all their inner strength to cope with the day to day needs of their children and to survive intact as a family unit.

10

Eventually, after obtaining legal aid, a Mr and Mrs Satherley issued a writ against DCBL on 7 November, on behalf of their son and themselves, alleging negligence. Issuing a writ makes a dispute *sub judice*, or subject to judicial determination, so that conduct prejudicial to a fair hearing of the case or liable to influence the outcome of negotiations would constitute a criminal contempt of court. It was by virtue of the *sub judice* rule that press comment on the case was then inhibited.

It was not until June 1966, nearly four years after the Satherleys had issued their writ, that court proceedings were in view and the Law Society authorised further legal aid to cover them. Why did it take so long to bring the thalidomide cases to trial, and why has the whole history of the litigation been so bedevilled by delay? Apart from the unavoidable administrative delays encountered in any legal system, several elements combined to prolong matters. The law relating to the case itself was far from certain. The complexity of the scientific and medical evidence necessitated a great deal of research and investigation. Initial uncertainty of diagnosis in many cases and the fact that the families were scattered throughout the country meant that isolated 'test' cases were begun, effectively preventing the emergence of a cohesive force capable of exerting any substantial pressure. No major initiative was forthcoming from Distillers. However, this does not necessarily imply that they lacked any sense of moral responsibility. A company also owes a duty to its shareholders not to deplete its funds unjustifiably. Even if this apparent conflict of interests could be resolved by concluding that a generous settlement was, as a matter of public relations, in the best long term interests of the company, a further complication would have been the nature of such insurance arrangements as the company had made, and the possibility of forfeiting its indemnity (a matter which, at the time of writing, is still in issue) by agreeing to settle on terms unacceptable to its insurers.

It is also reasonable to suppose that *neither* side really relished the prospect of a fully fought-out case. As Lord Justice Phillimore was to observe in *Attorney-General* v. *Times Newspapers Ltd*. (1973):

> ... I have no doubt that all this so-called litigation is somewhat unreal. No parent dares to bring one of these cases to trial for fear of losing, whilst Distillers are most unwilling to fight one of these cases lest they lose when, quite apart from the moral obloquy, the damages might well be enormous. In a sense we are dealing with something akin to shadow boxing dressed up as litigation.[10]

Many families faced a further difficulty over the time limit for commencing proceedings. A personal injuries action must normally be brought no later than three years 'from the date on which the cause of action accrued',[11] that is within three years of the damage occurring. In a case brought on behalf of a thalidomide child this would probably be construed to mean within three years of birth. Sixty-two writs were issued in time on behalf of deformed infants and their parents, alleging that DCBL were at fault in not carrying out adequate tests before marketing the drug.

It was evident that because of the complex issues involved litigation would be very expensive and might easily take two years with appeals. (The criminal proceedings in Germany against Chemie Grünenthal were finally abandoned eight and a half years after their inception, the continuation of the trial being deemed no longer in the public interest.) Leading counsel warned parents of the speculative nature of the claim, in view of the difficulty of establishing negligence by the manufacturers and the uncertainty as to whether a right of action existed in respect of an unborn child. Consequently a settlement was negotiated, which was formally approved by the High Court (as is mandatory where children are concerned) on 19 February 1968.

Under this settlement Distillers agreed to pay 40 per cent of the total amount to which each plaintiff would have been entitled if the company had been found liable, on condition that all allegations of negligence were unreservedly withdrawn, and that all sixty-two accepted. The two sides were to attempt to agree on the appropriate figure for the damages, failing which it would be determined by the court.

The parties were unable to agree on a figure and in July 1969 two cases were heard in the nature of representative actions. [12] In one, typifying the middle category of injured, the child was awarded £13,040 (i.e. £32,600 less 60 per cent), and his mother just under £2,900 (being £5,000 plus agreed damages for incurred expenses, less 60 per cent). The other child, who was in the most serious category of injured, received £20,800. The average award was £16,129; the total payment was almost £1 million. In the next chapter we shall consider how these amounts were arrived at. At this stage, suffice it to say that the judgement exemplified some of the features of the existing common law approach to the assessment of damages most open to criticism: the judge expressed regret that so much time had been taken up with questions of actuarial evidence, which he was to reject; he adopted the view – hardly realistic even in 1969 – that inflation and interest should be deemed to cancel each other out; a once-for-all sum was awarded, based on the somewhat primitive judicial approach to the assessment of damages for injury.

12

This settlement was confined to the sixty-two children on whose behalf actions had been brought within the statutory three-year period. In announcing it, counsel for the company gave an undertaking to the court that in view of the withdrawal of the allegations of negligence, it would consider making provision for the other malformed children. This statement was referred to by the Minister of Health when rejecting another request in Parliament for a public inquiry, on the grounds that he did not think that it could add significantly to what was already known.

The campaign against Distillers

Negotiations then began in order to settle the remaining claims, which seemed to be legally barred because of the limitation period. But the three-year time barrier is not invariable. The Limitation Act 1963 allowed a plaintiff to sue out of time in certain circumstances, and shortly after the settlement in February 1968 several other parents were exploring the possibility of commencing proceedings. On 5 July 1968 David Mason, who was to become the major spokesman for parents campaigning against Distillers, obtained leave to bring an action on rather technical grounds. Mrs Mason had not seen their daughter when she was born, and time did not run against a minor who, when her right of action accrued, was not 'in the custody of a parent'.[13] In other cases the parents had not been informed initially that their child's deformity was due to thalidomide, and time does not begin to run if the plaintiff is justifiably ignorant of 'material facts'.[14]

Eventually leave to sue out of time was granted to some 260 families, while a further 114 families were still pursuing their claim. Press and television coverage of thalidomide had dwindled. It had always focused on the consequences of the tragedy, because of the inhibiting *sub judice* rule. But towards the end of 1971 there were two significant developments. Several newspapers, partly at the instigation of David Mason, broadened the scope of their inquiries to consider the adequacy of the compensation resulting from the 1968 settlement. A new phase in the saga was about to begin, culminating in the protracted dispute between Distillers and *The Sunday Times* over the legitimate ambit of critical comment pending a court decision or settlement. Also, in November 1971 Distillers put forward a scheme to settle the outstanding claims by setting up a charitable trust fund of £3¼ million – on average about £8,500 per child – to be paid by instalments over ten years. In distributing the income the trustees would have 'due and proper regard for the differing needs and resources and for the differing degrees of handicap or disability suffered by individual beneficiaries'. But no lump sum was to be guaranteed for any child, the offer was conditional on acceptance by *all* the parents concerned, and it had to be kept confidential.

Not surprisingly, this proposal evoked a mixed reaction, reflecting the particular situation of individual families. Some would have preferred a standard lump sum for all instead of a discretionary trust. Many were disposed to accept rather than fight a speculative action, and others because they might not be granted leave to sue at all. Legal advisers for the parents visited various parts of the country explaining the implications of the trust deed. Those parents disinclined to go along with the offer were clearly faced with an intolerable dilemma. They were painfully aware that the vast majority could ill afford to turn down any offer which seemed substantial — if only in the short term — still less take their chance on protracted litigation in a matter that had already dragged on for nearly ten years.

It was later suggested by Mrs Barbara Castle in a House of Commons debate that certain parents had been 'threatened with the withdrawal of their legal aid certificates because they had refused to accept the advice of their solicitors to accept the settlement'.[15] There is in fact no evidence of any formal application having been made to a legal aid area committee, the only body entitled to withdraw a certificate, though the advice of their lawyers could no doubt have led some parents to fear that this might happen.

Distillers' all-or-nothing condition was bound to exert pressure on dissentients to accept the scheme, more especially as parents were asked at mass meetings with their legal advisers to indicate their views by a show of hands, in an atmosphere which, according to David Mason, was akin to a union meeting about a wage claim and hardly conducive to reasoned debate. Mason has written: 'I did not really relish joining argument against experienced counsel. I could feel the mood of acceptance in the hall, and I realised I could probably do nothing to change it. And I didn't fancy being booed. Or maybe lynched.'[16] At the same time, a means test would plainly be less advantageous to parents not in need of immediate compensation, who might also be more willing to pursue a claim through the courts, some of whom, like many other people, took exception to the idea that the children would be the objects of a charity set up by the very company which they saw as responsible. By this time it was also gradually emerging that some children in other countries such as Sweden, Canada, the United States and Germany were benefiting from more favourable settlements.

14

Indeed, had the company's offer of £3¼ million been accepted there and then, it would have amounted to a settlement representing roughly one-seventh of what was eventually achieved. It is worth dwelling for a moment on the background to the events immediately following, for they illustrate all too clearly how crucial chance factors and the involvement of the media proved in determining the outcome.

Mason, unlike the vast majority of thalidomide parents, was a successful businessman, whose keen appreciation of the economic realities was allied to a forceful personality. His resolve to obtain a substantially improved offer was fuelled by the belief that Distillers had reneged on a verbal undertaking given to his father (a shareholder in the company) that his daughter would be included in any settlement eventually reached. When the company excluded her, on the ground that her claim was defeated by the expiry of the limitation period, Mason, as we have seen, had to apply for leave to sue out of time. In the course of this application he rejected the opinion of a Queen's Counsel who advised against his chances, and obtained another barrister. Now that he wanted to stand out against the £3¼ million offer, he was again discouraged by his legal advisers, whom he promptly discharged.

At this juncture he sought to enlist the support of the media. He had a friend who knew the editor of *The Daily Mail*, which became the first newspaper to campaign actively on behalf of the children, printing three articles on successive days, beginning on 20 December 1971. Mason's determination caused him to retain and then discharge yet another firm of solicitors and two more Queen's Counsel. Convinced that following press exposure Distillers would not be able to continue what he regarded as moral blackmail, in insisting on 100 per cent acceptance, Mason proceeded to telephone all the other parents, discovering, after ten days of systematic inquiry, that four others were also prepared to resist. At the same time he heard from an American lawyer, who had read one of the *Daily Mail* articles, of a California Supreme Court decision in which one child was awarded the equivalent of £321,000.

In the end, then, five families held out, and one of the assenting parents sought to have the dissentients removed as 'next friend' (person bringing an action on behalf of a minor) and replaced by the Official Solicitor. This application succeeded initially, but in April 1972 the Court of Appeal reversed the decision on the ground that a parent as 'next friend' was entitled – perhaps even bound – to consider whether a proposed compromise was in the interests of his own child, without regard to the interests of any of the other children.[17] The court was also concerned that if it did permit the substitution of the Official Solicitor he would feel virtually obliged to accept the compromise on their behalf. Lord Denning stressed that if the whole settlement were jeopardised by their decision, this was a consequence of the company's condition and not of any unreasonableness on the part of the minority.

Though the campaign was far from being a one man effort, the part played by David Mason confronts us with some uncomfortable questions about the litigation process. How many litigants in a personal injury action would have had the money or temerity to discharge two leading firms of solicitors and three eminent counsel? How many would have taken part in a succession of press conferences, television and ·radio appearances, or would have had the kind of connections to make such a campaign seem feasible in the first place? How many individual litigants could even afford the time and money to contact some four hundred others? Mason has estimated that the campaign cost him £10,000 in expenses, £60,000 in business losses and about £40,000 on a particular transaction that he did not have the time to complete. How many people can afford the risk of an appeal after losing in the High Court? It would be invidious to attempt to judge between the conduct of the majority and that of the dissentients. But it remains deeply disturbing that the outcome of the dispute should have hinged so much on factors unrelated to the merits of the case.

Negotiations were resumed and in June 1972 Distillers put forward a new offer, which was not substantially different – a cash division of £2·9 million or the ten-year £3¼ million trust, provided this time that a 'substantial majority' agreed. This was not accepted and it was then that the campaign conducted by *The Sunday Times* began in earnest. On 24 September it published an article entitled 'Our Thalidomide Children: A Cause for National Shame', which it distributed to all members of both Houses of Parliament, and a leading article challenging the adequacy of Distillers' response:

> ... at the end of the day what is to be paid in settlement is the decision of Distillers, and they should offer much, much more to every one of the thalidomide victims. It may be argued that Distillers have·a duty to their shareholders and that, having taken account of skilled legal advice, the terms are just. But the law is not always the same as justice.

Despite Distillers' protests that this article constituted contempt, the Attorney-General refused to institute proceedings. But *The Sunday Times* then submitted for comment to the Attorney-General a further draft article, also sent to Distillers. This article purported to show that they had not exercised sufficient care to ensure that *Distaval* was safe before it was marketed. After a complaint from Distillers the Attorney-General applied for an injunction to prevent its publication, which was granted on 17 November.[18] The article was deemed to be part of a deliberate attempt 'to influence the settlement of pending proceedings by bringing pressure to bear on one party', which 'would create a serious risk of interference with Distillers' freedom of action in the litigation'. A week later, a television programme shown on 8 October was held not to have constituted contempt, on the ground that, as presented, it did not create a *serious* risk of such interference.[19]

By now the demand for a better settlement had reached massive proportions. It was reinforced by a poster campaign, in which several thousand posters mysteriously appeared on advertisements for Distillers' spirits. At the same time a committee was formed by some shareholders in the company, with a view to making it acknowledge moral responsibility for increased compensation. On 16 November, Jack Ashley, MP, a leading spokesman in Parliament on the children's behalf, said in the Commons: 'The primary aim of this campaign and debate is to help thalidomide children, who are a special case. I see them as a symbol of all disabled children. I hope that from their tragedy will emerge a will and a way of creating a new era for disabled children everywhere.' On 28 November, the day before the major debate in the Commons on the issue and the first reading of a private member's Bill to impose strict liability on manufacturers of unsafe drugs (expressed to be retroactive and to cover antenatal injuries), Distillers, whose profits for the previous half year had fallen by nearly £8 million, increased their offer from £3¼ million to £5 million. This would have represented about £13,500 per child, but in real terms it was only about two-thirds of the amount awarded to the sixty-two children in the 1968 settlement.

The Dangerous Drugs and Disabled Children Bill, introduced by Ron Lewis, MP, on 29 November 1972, was subsequently withdrawn, partly due to reservations expressed about anomalies resulting from piecemeal legislation responding to a particular situation. But it was also overtaken by events – the subsequent course of the negotiations and the Government's decision, in December, to set up a Royal Commission (the Pearson Commission), to investigate the whole field of civil liability and compensation for personal injury.[20]

The Commons debate on the same day[21] was notable for a spirited appeal by Jack Ashley for immediate action to compensate the children, coupled with his trenchant criticism of Distillers, while the Government maintained its stance of non-interference. Though it had agreed to make

£3 million available to supplement existing services for the congenitally disabled generally, it refused to set up a special fund for thalidomide children while negotiations were still in progress. Several MPs nevertheless expressed serious concern at the apparent inadequacy of legal procedures to bring matters to a satisfactory conclusion.

The scheme envisaged by Distillers was a trust fund which, if granted charitable status with tax relief, would over a period of ten years amount to £11·85 million, at a net cost to the company of £5 million. Each family would be offered an appropriate interest in the fund for its child. Ashley ridiculed these proposals: 'We must debate this offer now to show that Distillers is still acting as Scrooge, but now in the guise of Santa Claus'. He complained that the Government was being asked by the company to pass legislation conferring tax relief so that it could 'fob off its responsibilities on to the taxpayer'. David Mason said that he would ask Distillers' shareholders to petition for an extraordinary general meeting, with a view to obtaining an improved offer. On 19 December the Prime Minister announced the Government's decision to set up the Royal Commission on civil liability 'in the light of the Robens Report on Safety and Health at Work and the recent concern in connection with thalidomide children'. The Commission's terms of reference include 'death or personal injury (including ante-natal injury) suffered . . . through the manufacture, supply or use of goods or services'. We shall consider the remit of the Pearson Commission in chapter 5.

A settlement is reached

On 2 January 1973 Distillers were prompted to review their position. They had just received a letter from the Chancellor of the Exchequer, Anthony Barber, criticising them for stating in their formal offer of £5 million that '. . . there is reason to hope that the Government will be favourably disposed to a request for the assistance needed'. The offer, said Distillers, was made only on the assumption that tax relief would be granted for the fund.

However, by this time various developments seemed to herald an improved offer. The lobbying of the institutional investors and the Trades Union Congress was beginning to have an effect. Distillers was after all a company with 360 million issued shares, comprising some 250,000 holdings, including investment trusts, banks, local authorities, insurance companies, pension funds and professional associations. Pressure was brought to bear on the company by such influential insurance companies as the Prudential and the Legal and General. The Federation of Insurance Brokers pledged its support. Mason made a trip to the United States, where some 35 per cent of the company's profits are made, to see Ralph Nader, the consumer affairs expert, in the hope of achieving an American boycott, or at least the threat of one, while in England the Wrenson grocery chain actually did black Distillers' products. The merchant bankers, Schroder Wagg and Rothschilds, were trying to arrange a meeting between the management of Distillers and major institutional share-holders, who were becoming increasingly concerned at the threat posed to their investments by adverse publicity. The appeal against the injunction restraining *The Sunday Times* from publishing their article about the development, distribution and use of the drug was shortly to be heard.

The claimants' hopes were further boosted by the Australian decision in *Watt* v. *Rama*,[22] permitting a right of action in negligence for an unborn child who had suffered brain damage when its mother was injured in a car crash. Though English courts are never bound to apply Common-wealth law, they do sometimes attach weight to their decisions if English law on the matter is not settled. The decision might have helped the parents to overcome the preliminary hurdle of establishing the child's right to sue, especially if it were upheld at the appeal to the Privy Council expected to take place in March 1973. As it turned out the defendant did not appeal against the decision, but on 19 January 1973 the Law Commission was to publish a Working Paper, *Injuries to Unborn Children*,[23] also favouring such a right of action in principle. Moreover, further reports were being received of more advantageous settlements abroad.

On 5 January Distillers offered to increase the size of the trust fund from £11·85 million to £20 million. After meeting the institutional shareholders, the company issued a statement saying: '[We] cannot contemplate any increase in the sums now offered ... The increase in the sums provided by the new proposal does not indicate acceptance of any liability by the company'.

To examine the £20 million offer a working party was formed, headed by Jack Ashley and including representatives of the parents and the shareholders, as well as Harold Evans, editor of *The Sunday Times*. Distillers spelt out the full details of the new offer on 23 February. This was a week after the Court of Appeal had discharged the injunction that had prevented *The Sunday Times* from publishing its article, on the grounds that the litigation was dormant and that the public interest in discussion outweighed any prejudice it might cause.[24] The Attorney-General's request for leave to appeal to the House of Lords was refused by the Court of Appeal, but he appealed successfully against this refusal to the House of Lords itself and was later to win there.[25]

The new offer gave parents a choice of two methods of payment: (1) a lump sum of £5 million to be paid immediately, plus £1·5 million a year for ten years paid into a trust fund, or (2) a trust fund into which Distillers would pay £2 million a year for ten years. In either case there would also be an immediate cash payment of £5,000 to the parents – a total of £1·75 million. The company would also pay £20,000 a year for ten years towards operating the costs of the trust, plus 'reasonable' expenses of parents and their legal representatives.

Ashley recommended acceptance of one of these alternatives in principle, though he felt that payment ought to be over a five-year rather than ten-year period. Some fears were also expressed that the provisions for administration of the trust were insufficiently clear (for example, the procedure for assessing disabilities), and several parents, worried by the absence of any protection against inflation, felt that the immediate cash payment should be larger. Their legal advisers pressed Distillers further on these points and substantial improvements were made in April 1973.

The cash payment was to be increased to £6 million, or such additional amount needed to compensate the 340 or so outstanding cases who had so far received nothing, at the same rate as the 1968 group. The charitable trust fund would total £14 million, paid in at £2 million a year over seven years, to benefit *both* groups of children, and would be protected against inflation by a compound factor of up to 10 per cent annually. The parents would still receive the £5,000 payment. The overall result would be equivalent to cash settlements averaging about £54,000, a striking contrast to the 1972 offer (rejected by the dissenting five), which in real terms was worth only £7,500.

Ashley warmly welcomed the scheme and Mason commended it in principle. But when Distillers revealed further details on 5 May 1973, a new complication emerged. The offer was conditional on all the children being represented by Messrs Kimber, Bull and Company, who were to constitute the legal panel assessing disabilities and administering the fund. This was the London firm of solicitors which had represented many of the families which had settled in 1968, had encouraged acceptance of the £3¼ million offer and represented the majority in their attempt to have the five parents replaced as 'next friend'. There was some feeling that this involved the solicitors in a conflict of interests and in June one parent, Alec Purkis, complained to the Law Society who, after investigating the matter, replied in November that they were satisfied that his criticism was unfounded.

Mason suggested certain modifications to the scheme. He wanted the trust to be applied strictly on a points basis according to degree of disability, with no means test – the £6 million immediately; 80–90 per cent of the rest when the children were over eighteen, and the remaining 10–20 per cent to be kept in an emergency fund until the full effects of thalidomide became known, perhaps some fifteen to twenty years later. Ideally he wanted a sample survey to be conducted to assess the children's lifetime needs, but the parents' lawyers estimated that this would entail a further year's delay. Finally, he proposed that the disabilities should be assessed by a medical panel, as was to be the case in Australia, and not by lawyers. However, on 14 May 1973, at a meeting of some 300 parents, an informal vote in favour of accepting the company's offer was passed, whereupon Mason said he would end his campaign, on the understanding that the assessment panel would consider alterations to the mode of disposing of the funds.

But yet another difficulty was to present itself, which added strength to the view that the solicitors were placed in an invidious position. This was the problem of the 'X' list and the 'Y' list. On the X list were the 340 or so children accepted by Distillers as being thalidomide cases, whose financial interests would obviously be best served if the total number of claimants was not substantially increased. Early in June, Kimber, Bull revealed that there were 116 children on the Y list, that is, claimants not yet accepted by Distillers as genuine thalidomide cases. If many of them were promoted to the X list the cash equivalent of the offer would be reduced by several thousand pounds.

Meanwhile, in July, in the first contempt case directly affecting the press ever to reach it, the House of Lords reversed the decision of the Court of Appeal and reimposed the injunction forbidding *The Sunday Times* from publishing its article. The Lords took a restrictive view of the right to publish, holding that *any* prejudgement of the issues while litigation was pending amounted to contempt, seemingly even where there is no real risk of the court being influenced. The object, according to Lord Cross, was to prevent 'a gradual slide towards trial by newspaper or television'.[26]

Though the problem of the Y list could not, in the nature of things, be speedily resolved, the terms of the settlement proved acceptable to the vast majority of the parents and were finally sanctioned in the High Court on 30 July 1973 (in *Allen and Others* v. *DCBL*)[27] on behalf of 433 children. Its value was now virtually the equivalent of a settlement on a *full* liability basis, for the benefit of those children who were accepted by Distillers, or could satisfy a High Court judge that their disabilities were caused by the mother taking thalidomide. The fund was approved as a charitable trust, which it was assumed would exempt it from income tax and capital gains tax. A panel of seven lawyers would assess each child's claim, in the light of medical and social reports, with trial before a judge as a final resort if either a guardian or Distillers disputed the assessment. The lawyers involved agreed not to act for children who had not qualified and Distillers would pay the legal costs of parents seeking independent legal advice or a second opinion on the merits of the assessment.

It was of course part of the settlement that all allegations of negligence against Distillers were withdrawn. This effectively left the Y list children without any remedy unless they could manage to transfer to the X list, which by this time they might be unable to do for reasons wholly unconnected with the merits of their claim. The doctors concerned in several of the cases were either dead or untraceable, or lacked adequate records. The position of these families was far from enviable. Not only were they faced with great difficulty in establishing so long after the event that the mother had taken thalidomide at the relevant time, but also, however desirable it was that they should be represented by new solicitors, this inevitably meant that the complex chain of events had to be gone into all over again, and at a time when the impact of the campaign had receded. Since a few families refused to accept the offer, and parents of children on the Y list were still in dispute with the company, there was no question at this stage of the injunction against *The Sunday Times* being lifted. But as far as the general public was concerned the thalidomide issue was at an end.

The process of assessment, however, dragged on. Incredible as it may seem, in March 1974, almost one year after the final offer, and fifteen years after the birth of the first thalidomide child, a mere £150 was paid out of the trust to each child, because Kimber, Bull still lacked an overall account of the children's needs and disabilities. Thus medical panels had to start virtually from scratch to examine some 340 children, while the charitable trust also lacked the detailed information it needed about each child. Whereas Germany and Holland had exempted payments from tax and Japan, Australia and New Zealand planned to do the same, it was not yet clear whether parents receiving regular payments out of the trust would have to pay tax on it as 'income', despite the fact that they had accepted the offer in the belief that it would be exempt. As a result the investment plans of the trustees were also hampered.

By mid-1974 there were signs that the unconscionable delay was coming to an end. The medical and legal panels had finished examining the children on the X list and provisional assessments of each child's share were nearly complete. £500,000 had been paid out on account for cases in special need and the medical panel agreed to examine the remaining 95 children on the Y list. Payments from the £6 million capital fund for X list children were scheduled to begin in October 1974, but the tax issue was still unresolved.

The legal disputes over the right of *The Sunday Times* to publish their banned article on the making and marketing of the drug had become even more convoluted. After the decision in the House of Lords had gone against the newspaper, Harold Evans complained to the European Commission of Human Rights in Strasbourg that the British court's order violated Article 10 of the European Convention of Human Rights, which protects the right to freedom of expression. In May 1974 the Commission invited the United Kingdom government and *The Sunday Times* to submit their arguments on the question of the admissibility of the complaint. This is the first stage to be satisfied before any decision on whether there has been a violation may be made, and the complaint was later held to be admissible.

In the meantime another hurdle had appeared, one to which much less publicity has been given. The newspaper had always declared its confidence in the truth of the article. This turned out to be because the facts on which it was based came from Distillers' own documents. When the Satherleys brought the initial action against Distillers in 1962, the case reached the stage of discovery of documents, a process whereby parties disclose their evidence, which they may then be compelled by the court to reveal to the other side. Some 10,000 documents reached the claimants in this way. The documents were given to a chemist retained to advise the parents, Dr Montague Phillips. Phillips approached *The Sunday Times*, and Harold Evans later concluded an agreement with him under which he was to be paid £5,000 for documentary and other information he would supply. Phillips allowed *The Sunday Times* to photocopy the discovery documents, as Distillers found out only when they were shown a draft of the article eventually found to be in contempt. At first *The Sunday Times* undertook not to publish it but in March 1974 they revoked this undertaking, and Distillers immediately applied to the court for an injunction restraining the disclosure or use of their documents. A judge in the High Court granted the injunction on the grounds that (1) documents disclosed on discovery should, as a matter of public interest, enjoy the protection of the court against any unauthorised use unrelated to the action in which they were disclosed; (2) the proposed use of the documents had not been shown to be of greater benefit to the public than its interest in protecting their confidentiality; (3) arguably the use of the documents would also be

23

in breach of copyright law.[28] These obstacles to the publication of the banned article may be impossible to surmount. However the contempt obstacle was removed on 23 June 1976 when the Divisional Court, on the Attorney-General's application, ruled that three years after the settlement it was no longer necessary to restrain comment, since none of the four cases technically still outstanding were in fact being actively pursued. *The Sunday Times* was thereby enabled to publish on 27 June a six-page account of the thalidomide story, but a partial account only, in view of the continuing ban on use of Distillers' documents.

Changes in the law of contempt will probably come. In December 1974 the Phillimore Committee reported.[29] The Committee was much influenced by the whole history of the thalidomide litigation, and its recommendations, if enacted, would considerably extend the right to publish.

Assessing the situation on 16 November 1975, exactly three years after the High Court injunction restraining publication, *The Sunday Times* expressed considerable satisfaction and optimism. A Treasury ruling in October 1974 refusing tax exemption on the income from the trust prompted an outcry in the press and led to renewed efforts by Jack Ashley and some of the parents. The problem was eventually resolved by the Government authorising the payment of £5 million to the trust, so as to offset the effects of taxation without having to change the law. Also the Inland Revenue was prepared to exempt from tax funds used in buying or making alterations to houses. The work of the medical and legal panels was almost complete. Of 410 known cases, in only seven was a preliminary assessment yet to be made.[30] The 10 per cent compound inflation factor had considerably eased the task of the trustees and, most importantly, many of the adolescent children were beginning to cope effectively with their physical and psychological disabilities. In no small measure was this due to the substantially increased sums obtained.

On the litigation front there remains the intriguing question of Distillers' rights, if any, against its insurers. Calculations made in 1974 showed that the company's potential liability was not £20 million as originally estimated but, primarily because of inflation, £28.4 million. In theory Distillers had insurance cover, but its insurers have disclaimed liability, alleging that the company failed to disclose relevant facts *and that they did not carry out adequate tests and research on the drug.* Distillers have sued the underwriters and the case was set down for 4 October 1976. It would be an ironic twist indeed to this complex and protracted series of legal battles if the very issues which *The Sunday*

Times has sought to have fully aired in public are finally litigated for no other reason than Distillers' attempt to enforce its contract of insurance.

Notes

[1]   See the Poisons List Order, 1960, no. 698, 7 April 1960.

[2]   See H. Sjöström and R. Nilsson, *Thalidomide and the Power of the Drug Companies*, Penguin 1972, p. 194. Several of the factual details in this chapter are derived from this work.

[3]   H. Taussig, 'A Study of the German Outbreak of Phocomelia', *Journal of the American Medical Association*, 1962, p. 1106.

[4]   A. Birch-Jensen, *Congenital Deformities of the Upper Extremities*, Munksgaard (Copenhagen) 1950.

[5]   See M. Mintz, *The Therapeutic Nightmare*, Houghton 1965, ch. 12.

[6]   *Thalidomide and the Power of the Drug Companies*, p. 106.

[7]   Ibid., p. 106. Letter to Dr C.N. Brown, 11 December 1961.

[8]   *The Pharmaceutical Journal* (editorial), vol. 188, 1962, p.109.

[9]   See generally *The Thalidomide Children and the Law*, a report by *The Sunday Times*, André Deutsch 1973.

[10]   [1973] Q.B.710, 743.

[11]   Limitation Act 1939, s.2(1)(a), as amended by the Law Reform (Limitation of Actions, etc.) Act 1954 and the Limitation Act 1975.

[12]   *S.* v. *Distillers Co. (Biochemicals)* [1969] 3 All E.R. 1412.

[13]   See now Limitation Act 1975, s.2.

[14]   See now Limitation Act 1975, s.1.

[15]   H.C. Deb. vol. 847, col. 452, 29 November 1972.

[16]   D. Mason, *Thalidomide: My Fight,* Allen and Unwin 1976, p. 49.

[17]   *In re Taylor's Application* [1972] 2 Q.B.369.

[18]   *Attorney-General* v. *Times Newspapers Ltd.* [1972] 3 All E.R.1136.

[19]   *Attorney-General* v. *London Weekend Television* [1972] 3 All E.R. 1146.

[20]   H.C. Deb. vol. 848, col. 1119, 19 December 1972.

[21]   H.C. Deb. vol. 847, cols. 432–509, 29 November 1972.

[22]   *Watt* v. *Rama* [1972] V.R.353.

[23]   Working Paper no. 47, 19 January 1973.

[24]   *Attorney-General* v. *Times Newspapers Ltd.* [1973] 1.Q.B.710.

[25]   *Attorney-General* v. *Times Newspapers Ltd.* [1974] A.C.273.

[26] Ibid., p.323.

[27] *Allen and Others* v. *Distillers Co. (Biochemicals) Ltd.* [1974] 2 All E.R.365.

[28] *Distillers Co. (Biochemicals) Ltd.* v. *Times Newspapers Ltd.* [1975] 1 All E.R.41.

[29] *Report of the Committee on Contempt of Court*, HMSO 1974, Cmnd. 5794.

[30] As regards the Y list, by July 1976 Distillers had accepted a further twelve cases, which left eighty-six children, twenty-four of whom have discontinued their claims.

2 The legal issues:1 liability and compensation

In the actions brought in 1968 a settlement was reached under which Distillers agreed to pay each claimant 40 per cent of the damages which would have been recovered had liability been established. What then were the obstacles to proof of the company's legal liability?

The meaning of negligence in law

The branch of English civil law concerned with the right of an injured person to compensation is known as the law of torts. Nowadays the overwhelming majority of personal injury actions are based on the tort of negligence, which may be defined as the breach of a legal duty to take care which results in damage. The question of the company's liability centred on three key issues. First, did thalidomide cause the damage? Secondly, were Distillers negligent in law in marketing the drug? Thirdly, does a person have a right to sue for damage done to him before his birth?

The first of these questions need not detain us. Whatever uncertainty there may have been initially, the incidence of foetal deformity when thalidomide was available, combined with the subsequent tests revealing teratogenic effects (i.e. causing congenital deformity) on animals, has established that the drug could and did cause damage of this kind. The other two issues are more problematic.

The concept of the duty of care is necessarily fluid and has been widened considerably in recent years, but a natural starting-point remains the classic exposition in *Donoghue* v. *Stevenson* (1932).[1] In that case Lord Atkin formulated his famous 'neighbour principle' in the following terms:

> You must take reasonable care to avoid acts or omissions which you can reasonably foresee would be likely to injure your neighbour. Who, then, in law is my neighbour? The answer seems to be — persons who are so closely and directly affected by my act that I ought reasonably to have them in contemplation as being so affected when I am directing my mind to the acts or omissions which are called in question.

This statement of general principle is far from being definitive of what constitutes negligence in law, but it has exercised enormous influence, to such an extent that in *Home Office* v. *Dorset Yacht Co. Ltd.* (1970)[2] Lord Reid felt able to say '. . . I think the time has come when we can and should say that it ought to apply unless there is some justification or valid explanation for its exclusion'.

The primary test of liability then is reasonable foreseeability that your careless conduct will cause injury. But it has long been apparent that the superficial objectivity of this approach obscures what are often in reality policy decisions, involving additional or alternative criteria. In particular the courts are disposed to take account of the degree of probability that injury will result from the defendant's conduct; the potential magnitude of the injury in a given case; the value to the community of the defendant's conduct or enterprise; the burden which taking adequate precautions would impose on him, and the danger of the courts being inundated with claims of a similar kind.

In other words, the issue is not always confined to whether X ought reasonably to have foreseen that his conduct would injure Y, but may entail considering where the balance of *social* interest lies. Not surprisingly, in the nineteenth century the courts were usually in favour of X carrying on his activities with a minimum of constraint. In the early development of negligence as a separate tort in the wake of the industrial revolution, fears that enterprise would be stifled by excessive accident claims were reflected in stringent requirements of proof of fault, and various devices were developed either to limit the range of liability or to deny it outright.[3]

In today's changed social and economic climate the balance of social interest is seen in a different light. The existence of insurance on a large scale has in practice softened the financial consequences to enterprise of a finding of negligence. The judiciary is correspondingly more disposed to acknowledge the relevance of criteria other than foreseeability. Thus Lord Pearce observed in *Hedley Byrne & Co. Ltd.* v. *Heller & Partners Ltd.* (1964)[4]: 'How wide the sphere of the duty of care is to be laid depends ultimately on the courts' assessment of the *demands of society* for protection from the carelessness of others'.

Negligence in relation to defective products

Harm through negligence may arise in any number of different ways, ranging from physical injury caused by a careless driver to financial loss resulting from reliance on careless words. The nature of the harm will in part determine the relevant criteria of liability and our particular concern is with how the law has developed in respect of injury caused by the marketing of defective – that is unsafe – products. The leading case of *Donoghue* v. *Stevenson* (where injury was allegedly caused by the presence of a snail in a ginger beer bottle) is thus singularly appropriate for our purpose, as appears from the central proposition which it lays down:

> . . . the manufacturer of an article of food, medicine or the like, sold by him to a distributor in circumstances which prevent the distributor or the ultimate purchaser or consumer from discovering by inspection any defect, is under a legal duty to the ultimate purchaser or consumer to take reasonable care that the article is free from defect likely to cause injury to health.[5]

It is clear from several cases after *Donoghue* v. *Stevenson* that in actions brought by consumers against manufacturers the courts will readily infer negligence if satisfied that a defect arising from error or carelessness in the process of manufacture caused the injury.[6] This remains true even where the defendant has taken reasonable care in his general process of manufacture. Because the number of potential claimants is so large when goods are marketed, the criterion of magnitude of risk assumes unusual importance. As Weir points out, under the guise of a negligence approach we have imposed on manufacturers what is often tantamount to the strict liability of a guarantor.[7]

To understand why a drug such as thalidomide does not automatically attract such a 'guarantor's liability', it must be appreciated that what is at issue here is not some error in the process of manufacture, but an error of design. There may be a defect in design when the product is under the actual control of the manufacturer. Alternatively, it may arise at an earlier stage, if he is making use of a formula supplied by a third party. Even in the latter situation it would seem that the manufacturer is potentially liable, quite independently of any right of action the injured person may have against the supplier.[8] But in neither case will the manufacturer be liable if the design itself could not be faulted in the light of scientific or technical knowledge current when the product was marketed. Whatever view the court might take as to the burden of proof, it would still be open to the manufacturer, as happened in the abortive German criminal proceedings, to mount a highly technical case, asserting the adequacy of his safety precautions and testing procedures.

It should be stressed that our main focus at this stage is on the potential liability of a manufacturer in negligence, because in English law this was the most plausible way of formulating the children's claim. In many American States a consumer injured by a defective product may succeed without having to prove negligence, provided he can show that the defect arose before the product left the manufacturer. He might also, even where he has not bought the product, be able to pursue what are in essence contractual remedies against the manufacturer. By comparison with English and most Commonwealth law, these alternatives are more in accord with economic reality, in that the manufacturer typically distributes accident losses in pricing his goods and taking out insurance. They also conform more closely to the notion of a 'guarantor's liability', as expressing the moral obligation of a company which through its advertising attempts to reach the public at large. However, whether they provide superior remedies in the particular context of prescribed drugs we shall consider in chapter 5.

A child's claim against the manufacturer

Could a thalidomide child have succeeded in negligence against Distillers? To appreciate the range and complexity of analysis implicit in this simple-sounding question one cannot do better than list the sixteen questions which counsel for *The Sunday Times* in the case about discovery documents, *Distillers* v. *Times Newspapers* (1975), [9] suggested were relevant to an investigation of the tragedy:

> [the questions] involve the general state of scientific knowledge from 1956 to 1958, the knowledge and experience of Chemie Grünenthal, the reliance placed by the plaintiffs [in this context Distillers] on that company, the tests carried out by the plaintiffs and their research into medical and scientific literature, the obtaining of clinical reports and whether the plaintiffs exercised influence on those making reports, the plaintiff's knowledge at each stage, the experience and strength of their staff and their facilities, the steps taken by the plaintiffs to keep the medical profession and the people informed, whether the views of the plaintiffs' medical and scientific staff were subordinated to the management and sales staff's views. what part commercial considerations played in the marketing and advertising, steps taken by the plaintiffs to ensure that adverse reports reached them, the date when the plaintiffs and DCBL first learned of teratogenic births, the responsibility of a multi-national company for its subsidiary, what discussions the plaintiffs had with

the Ministry of Health and, finally, why no public inquiry has been held.

Distillers manufactured as well as distributed *Distaval*, under licence from Chemie Grünenthal, the original manufacturers. What bearing would this have on Distillers' liability, if any, in negligence? On the hypothesis that Chemie Grünenthal were themselves negligent, reliance by Distillers on them could only operate as a defence if a manufacturer cannot be held legally responsible for adopting a third party's negligent design. There is a surprising lack of direct authority on this point in English law, but the consensus of opinion is that there can be liability of this kind.[10] As Greig points out:

> For *Donoghue* v. *Stevenson* to operate satisfactorily in the increasingly complex world of modern industrial processes, it is obvious that it must be applicable against the ostensible manufacturers, i.e. the person who brings all the component parts together as the finished product. He will therefore be liable for a defect arising at any stage in the manufacturing processes, whether through his own carelessness or that of his supplier.[11]

This argument is reinforced by the fact that Distillers carried out their own additional toxicity tests.

But even if Distillers could in principle be liable as manufacturers, they would only be liable in law if they were (or, arguably, if Chemie Grünenthal had been)[12] negligent in not discovering that the design was defective, or in failing to withdraw the drug as soon as they found out. Much of the controversy hinges on whether the tests carried out were adequate to discharge Distillers' duty of care. The primary criterion remains that of reasonable foreseeability, which here implies taking such precautions as could be expected from a prudent drug manufacturer in the light of medical and scientific knowledge available when the drug was being marketed.[13]

It is important to note at this point that careless conduct (or omission) will not of itself constitute negligence in law. It has to be shown that the carelessness was an *operative* cause of the injury. In one case[14] where a doctor was found to be 'negligent' in not seeing a patient who subsequently died it was held that because there was no reasonable prospect of the patient being diagnosed and treated in time to save him in any event, the doctor could not be found liable in negligence. Similarly, to establish liability against Distillers it would not suffice to show that it was 'negligent' not to have carried out teratogenicity tests, unless, on a balance of probabilities, properly conducted tests of this nature would have revealed the dangers.

What then was the state of medical and scientific knowledge at the relevant time, and how probative would such tests have been? Medical and scientific opinion is sharply divided. The arguments may be summarised as follows. Those who claim that the absence of teratogenicity tests did not amount to negligence might argue that such tests were not part of standard screening procedure in 1958, at all events for drugs like thalidomide: 'The discovery that thalidomide, a pharmacodynamic drug, produces congenital malformations was a shock, since these effects had previously been associated only with substances that interfere with the synthesis of protein and nucleic acids'.[15] They could also point to the practical difficulties and doubtful value of much of this testing on laboratory animals, due to the great variability of effects. There are several reasons for this variability. The foetus is only sensitive to such substances in early pregnancy and only seriously vulnerable for a limited time span within that period, which itself varies from one animal to another and even in different species of a given animal. Thus although numerous species of rabbits were subsequently tested it seems that only the foetus of the New Zealand white rabbit was shown to be susceptible in the same way as the human foetus. Also, within the spectrum of activity of any teratogenic agent there is a relatively narrow band of dosage which is capable of producing deformed young.

Lastly it should be remembered that teratogenic experiments in animals can never prove the existence of such effects in humans and that extrapolation from one to the other is always conjectural. Ironically in the aftermath of the tragedy penicillin was found to produce teratogenic effects in some animal species, though not in man. Of course, the limitations of animal tests in predicting effects on the human embryo also support the case for not advertising *any* new drugs for use by pregnant women, but we shall return to that point later.

The case *for* negligence would stress the extent to which pharmacologists were already aware of teratogenic dangers in general. In 1934 a doctor wrote:

> That the placenta is permeable to drugs has long been recognised. The obstetrician has for many years accepted this fact and since it has become recognised that quinine, when administered to the mother, may be toxic to the foetus much research work has been done on the subject.[16]

In 1946 a long term study was begun at the Columbia Presbyterian

Medical Center in New York to study the frequency and causes of foetal death and malformation among a sample of the population. By 1958 it was known that several hundred chemicals had been shown experimentally to be capable of producing congenital deformity. Many responsible pharmaceutical concerns in the 1950s conducted full investigations of the possible deleterious action of new drugs on the foetus. As early as 1950, *Daraprim*, an anti-malarial drug developed by Burroughs-Wellcome, was tested on rats for teratogenic effects. So too, in 1953–54, was *Miltown*, a tranquilliser produced by Wallace Laboratories and subsequently marketed by Chemie Grünenthal in Germany. Substantial doses of thalidomide administered to pregnant rats causes resorption (a chemically induced abortion). If such testing had been carried out, the consequent decline in litter size, while not probative as to the effect on humans, might at least have served as a warning signal meriting further investigation. When Smith, Kline and French proposed to put the tranquilliser *Prochlorperazine* on the market in 1956, to be used for the treatment of nausea during pregnancy, they tested with animals for its effects on the foetus. CIBA did likewise with *Doriden* in 1959. Thalidomide was not produced by one of the larger drug concerns such as these. Chemie Grünenthal was an offshoot of a German soap manufacturer, formed to profit from the antibiotic boom in post-war Germany. The Distillers company too was more renowned for other products and has since abandoned its interest in the pharmaceutical field.

By 1958 it was also known with a considerable degree of precision at what stage of organogenesis (the formation of limbs and organs) of a given species the dangers were greatest. According to Woollam: 'Morning sickness [for which thalidomide was prescribed] is likely to be most troublesome just at the very time when the foetus is most at risk'.[17] He further maintains that a series of tests on mice, rats and rabbits, under varying conditions of timing and dosage 'would almost certainly have revealed the teratogenic properties of thalidomide'.[18] Lesser points out that it was precisely because of our accumulated knowledge in the field that 'within five months of its being withdrawn from the market, thalidomide could be proved to produce deformity of the newborn of rabbits, and within a year of rats and mice'.[19] Later experiments on monkeys produced malformations remarkably similar to those in humans.

Chemie Grünenthal tested thalidomide on animals (though not for teratogenicity), but at the trial in Germany it transpired that many of the records of these tests had been destroyed or lost. Sjöström and Nilsson go so far as to say that: 'Thalidomide was introduced according to the method of Russian roulette. Practically nothing was known about several aspects of this new drug at the time of its marketing'.[20] The cautiousness of the Food and Drug Administration in the United States serves as an example to other countries. A memorandum from the FDA's official files[21] reveals that for more than a year Dr Frances Kelsey resisted persistent attempts by Richardson-Merrell to obtain a licence for the American market. She was not satisfied that enough cases had been studied or that the data submitted based on clinical trials in Germany and America was sufficiently detailed about safety, adverse effects and chronic toxicity. Her own student research had been on the effects of drugs on the foetus, and she also sought evidence as to whether thalidomide·might be harmful in this respect.

To attempt to judge between the two conflicting views of the matter would require not only advanced scientific expertise, but also the very investigation in depth of the whole process of testing and marketing the drug which has never been undertaken. In default of such evidence, dogmatic assertions on either side are out of place. Certainly the state of medical knowledge and practice current then are highly important guides to the standard of care required. If a court took the view that the company could not have anticipated injury to the foetus in the first place, it could perfectly properly dispose of the case on that footing, and the positive assertion that the drug was perfectly safe for pregnant women would not imply the rashness which, with hindsight, it suggests. As Lord Denning observed in *Roe* v. *Minister of Health* (1954): 'We must not look at the 1947 accident with 1954 spectacles'. [22]

But current practice is not necessarily conclusive. If expert evidence suggested that even a slight risk of foetal deformity should have been foreseen, the flexibility of the law on negligence and the willingness of the courts to entertain policy considerations in this area would allow some scope for exacting a higher standard of care from the defendants than is implied in a straightforward application of the reasonable foreseeability test. For we would then be concerned with potentially grave harm to a vulnerable section of the community. [23] Pregnant women are after all particularly prone to take sedatives and were envisaged as one market for the drug. It is instructive to note the reasoning of the House of Lords in *Haley* v. *LEB* (1965) [24] in this respect. The defendants were excavating a trench in the street and took precautions which were adequate to warn sighted persons, but inadequate for a blind person, such as the plaintiff, who was injured in consequence. The court held that the number of blind persons who go about the streets unaided is sufficient to require the defendants to have them in contemplation and to take precautions appropriate to their condition. Positively recommending thalidomide for pregnant women would arguably imply a duty to carry out the only kind of acceptable testing – on pregnant animals – which might (though only might) have revealed the potential dangers.

An added argument on policy grounds for exacting a high standard of care before marketing relates to the purpose which the particular drug was meant to serve. There is a case for saying that safety requirements need to be especially stringent for a mere sedative, intended for a variety of relatively minor conditions in children and adults, particularly when there are safe alternatives on the market. On the other hand, a court might also be influenced by a competing social interest, namely the utility of the pharmaceutical industry in general and how it might be affected by the burden of taking extra precautions; that is the degree to which innovation could be inhibited by extra cost, and delay prevent valuable products from reaching the market at the earliest possible opportunity.

The policy arguments then do not all point in the same direction. Above all, it bears repeating that even if a court were persuaded that in all the circumstances the testing actually carried out was inadequate, it would not find negligence unless satisfied as to the probability that more acceptable testing would have revealed the defective nature of the drug.

The formidable obstacle for the plaintiff of showing precisely how the defect arose has in practice sometimes led the courts to shift the burden of proof on to the manufacturer, so that he has the onus of *disproving* negligence, or at least of providing a plausible explanation of how the damage could have occurred without his negligence.

Would this so-called doctrine of *res ipsa loquitur* ('the thing speaks for itself') provide a short cut to a finding of liability? It has sometimes been argued that this willingness of the courts to infer negligence when defective goods are marketed has all but nullified the negligence concept, so that liability is strict, being imposed even in the absence of negligence, provided only that the goods were defective when they left the manufacturer. But this is to over-simplify the issue in a legal system in which many judges will approach consumer claims predominantly from the standpoint that individual fault has to be proved.

The precise status and effect of *res ipsa loquitur* in English case law is far from settled.[25] Its applicability was denied both in *Donoghue* v. *Stevenson* itself and even in later cases where it seems nonetheless to have been relied on.[26] More importantly, the courts have alternated between regarding it as a distinct rule of law totally shifting the burden of proof so that the manufacturer would have to *disprove* negligence, or, and this seems to be the prevailing view,[27] permitting him to satisfy the onus with a mere explanation, consistent with the facts, of how the damage could have occurred without his negligence. But even if the courts were consistently to burden the manufacturer with the heavier 'onus of disproof', it would not remove a most serious obstacle to a plaintiff in a technically complex negligence dispute such as thalidomide, namely the ability of a powerful defendant to compel settlement on terms unfavourable to someone who cannot take the risks or endure the delay which *any* investigation of that issue might involve.

In considering the circumstances in which marketing a harmful drug could attract negligence liability we have so far emphasised the legal implications of inadequate testing. But it is artificial to look at this aspect in isolation. One must examine the total process of marketing the drug, including the promptness with which the company publicises dangers once they are known and the steps it takes to withdraw a drug from the market where necessary. Undue delay in these respects would amount to negligence, even if the original marketing did not.

Precisely when such duties arise is always a question of fact, though not one which is necessarily easy to determine. It will depend on such matters as the reliability of the reports of adverse effects, their extent and severity, the availability of safe alternative remedies, the efficacy and overall value of the suspect drug and the relative seriousness of the condition for which it is being prescribed.

In the case of thalidomide, the relatively triviality of the conditions it was designed to alleviate, the existence of several adequate alternatives and the catastrophic nature of the reported teratogenic effects, clearly indicated the need for very prompt disclosure and withdrawal. Distillers may have acted with due dispatch by taking steps to withdraw the drug and inform the medical profession as soon as they received firm reports of the findings of Dr Lenz and Dr McBride towards the end of November 1961. On the other hand, Dr McBride's suspicions about teratogenicity were made known to the Australian subsidiary of Distillers in June 1961. The precise course of events in the intervening months remains somewhat obscure, as is apparent from the *Sunday Times* attempt to piece together what happened, in its article of 27 June 1976. The fact that between June and September twenty-three mothers who had taken *Distaval* had normal births may have convinced the Australian branch that McBride was mistaken, since they would not have appreciated at that time that the drug could cause malformations only if taken between the fifth and eighth week of pregnancy. The task of distinguishing between excusable delay and negligence is further complicated by having to rely on faded recollections of what happened many years previously, when the

36

participants had no reason to suppose that the exact sequence of events might be of importance.

Also problematic is the importance to be attached to the way in which the drug was promoted and advertised in the first place. We have already drawn attention to the bitter irony revealed in the wording of Distillers' advertisements for thalidomide, but its precise legal significance is not easy to assess. A major reason for this difficulty is the law's traditional reluctance to impose liability as readily for careless words as for careless conduct. While it is not always easy to find any logical justification for the distinction, it is not difficult to appreciate why it has arisen. Words typically have less impact than deeds. They cause injury in a less direct way since unlike, for example, negligent driving, no harm results from them alone. The injured party must first act in consequence of them. Also, people are often less careful about what they say than about what they do, so that judges have stressed the danger of chance careless remarks opening up the 'floodgates of litigation', a favourite judicial argument when legal reforms are mooted.

It was for example not until 1963[28] that liability in tort for negligent misstatement causing *financial* loss was recognised at all, and even now its range of application is quite limited, requiring some pre-existing 'special relationship' between plaintiff and defendant. However, our concern is with allegedly negligent statements and *physical* injury, and while in such cases the courts retain a measure of caution since words, not deeds, are the cause, they are willing to recognise a duty of care in such circumstances. As Fleming puts it:

> ... the range of protected persons is here far less restricted [than in the case of words causing financial loss] ... Anyone in fact may qualify who, in consonance with the conventional criterion for physical injury, was likely to be harmed as the result of the defendant's negligent statement, *no matter seemingly whether it be communicated to him directly or influence someone else to pursue a course of action perilous to him.* Thus it does not appear necessary for the plaintiff to have been personally identified in advance as someone likely to place justifiable reliance on the communication for the purpose of a specific transaction, as this is understood in the context of pecuniary damage.[29]

That this line of reasoning is relevant to thalidomide is demonstrated by yet another of those tantalising cases where the negligence issue was formulated but not litigated — the Privy Council decision of *Distillers Co.*

(Biochemicals) Ltd. v. *Thompson* (1971). [30] The point at issue was the preliminary one of jurisdiction. Did a thalidomide victim have the right to sue DCBL (who manufactured the drug in England and supplied it to its Australian subsidiary) in New South Wales, where the mother obtained it from a chemist, if the injury occurred there? Under New South Wales law, the court has a discretion to exercise jurisdiction over a non-resident (such as DCBL) if 'there is a cause of action which arose within the jurisdiction'.[31] This meant that DCBL could not be sued in New South Wales if the assumed operative negligence was the *manufacture* of the drug. Only if it were the *failure to warn* of the dangers did the Australian court have the right to hear the case.

In the New South Wales Court of Appeal,[32] Holmes J.A. expressed the issue as follows:

> This is not a case of careless manufacture. The Distival [sic] in this case for all one knows or is ever likely to know was no different from the other Distival manufactured by the appellant. Indeed it is not put that there was an act, neglect, or default in the manufacture of the Distival, but that the breach of duty by the manufacturer was the failure to warn the pregnant purchaser. This was the breach of duty which was, it is said, causally connected with the damage to the plaintiff.

In upholding this view of jurisdiction the Privy Council said:

> ... that warning might have been given by putting a warning notice on each package as it was made up in England. It could also have been given by communication to persons in New South Wales – the medical practitioners, the wholesale and retail chemists, patients and purchasers. The plaintiff is entitled to complain of the lack of such communication in New South Wales as negligence by the defendant in New South Wales causing injury to the plaintiff there. That is the act (which must include omission) on the part of the English company which has given the plaintiff a cause of complaint in law.[33]

It will be noticed that the Privy Council characterised the failure to warn as 'the *act* (which must include omission)'. In other words, the failure to issue warnings could in principle constitute the operative negligence. As Winfield and Jolowicz put it:

> ... many cases of negligence which have never been regarded as raising the problem of misrepresentation nevertheless contain as an

essential element in the sequence of events a misrepresentation, express or, more commonly, implied ... there are cases in which the distinction between word and deed is for all practical purposes non-existent. Quite apart from contract, a doctor is as much liable for negligently advising his patient to take a certain drug as he is for negligently injecting the drug himself.[34]

There is authority for the proposition that where a manufacturer *knows* of the potential danger of his product he has a duty to see that an adequate warning is displayed.[35] By the same token, when he makes bold assertions as to its safety, he may be required to take correspondingly greater precautions if he is to avoid liability for negligence when it proves to be unsafe. This is illustrated by the case of *Watson* v. *Buckley* (1940), where the plaintiff successfully sued the distributors of a dangerous hair dye who had advertised it as 'the safe harmless hair dye'. Mr Justice Stable observed:

> Before committing their name to such an assertion to all and sundry, they should have taken far greater care to ensure that that assertion was based on solid ground. ... The negligent acts of the distributor were the various acts and omissions and representations which intervened between the manufacture of the article and its reaching [the plaintiff].[36]

It is true that in this case the plaintiff had actually read and been influenced by the advertisement, and that no tests at all had been carried out. But the important point for our purposes is that the assertions of safety in the advertisements of a mere distributor were deemed relevant to the standard of care reasonably to be expected.

In the United States, where the marketing of drugs is often accompanied by extensive and vigorous promotional campaigns, the negligence liability of manufacturers has in several recent cases been based on the totality of their promotional efforts.[37] This development highlights the artificiality of divorcing the act of marketing a product from the positive claims made about it. When one bears in mind the dangers of drugs as commodities in general and the relatively expert status of a drug manufacturer in their preparation,[38] common sense suggests that it is highly unsatisfactory to advertise a drug as 'perfectly harmless for pregnant women' without attempting to substantiate this claim. But the logical difficulty remains: unless the manufacturers knew or ought to have known of the risk they were, *ex hypothesi*, under no duty to warn. On the face of it, a positive recommendation seems more reprehensible than a failure to warn, but it is difficult to see how this would affect the appropriate legal principle in this context. Even in the absence of such advertising it is submitted that pregnant women would have been a foreseeable class of users of the sedative. At most the company's claims for thalidomide's safety merely reinforce the view that it should have been tested on pregnant animals.

The unborn child

The other major issue in an action by the children against the manufacturers was whether or not a right of action existed in respect of ante-natal injury. There was no authoritative English case law on this point, though for several other purposes the law had recognised the rights of the unborn child. A child *en ventre sa mère* is protected in respect of inherited interests in property[39] and, under the Fatal Accidents Acts, is deemed to be a 'child' for the purpose of receiving compensation for the death of a parent.[40] It would surely be anomalous if his physical well-being were seen as less worthy of protection. As Mr Justice Hiemstra observed in *Pinchin* v. *Santam* (1963),[41] a South African case concerning a child born with cerebral palsy caused by injury to the pregnant mother: 'If one can visualise a mind so evil as to allow the intentional administration of a drug like thalidomide, in order to produce a misshapen infant, our law would be archaic and inflexible if it should refuse an action'.

Early common law authorities denied any right of action for two main reasons. In the first reported American decision, *Dietrich* v. *Northampton* (1884),[42] Mr Justice Holmes held that as the child was part of its mother it had no independent legal personality. A nineteenth century Irish case, *Walker* v. *Great Northern Railway Company of Ireland* (1891),[43] was strongly influenced by what we would now see as misplaced fears about the technical difficulties of proving causation and the dangers of fraudulent claims. This is not to deny that many instances of ante-natal injury will give rise to problems of causation – even in the case of thalidomide there are the children on the Y list – but difficulties of proof in particular cases do not provide a convincing reason for denying a remedy in principle.

No doubt reluctance to recognise a right of action was also bound up with the belief that it would imply that the foetus *itself* has a legal personality, with all the attendant implications this could have for abortion. But there is no need to draw this conclusion. There is nothing really mysterious about asserting that the right of action belongs to the

40

child and crystallises on birth. If one reverts to basic principles of the law of negligence, the key issue, as perceived in the Australian case of *Watt* v. *Rama* (1972),[44] is simply whether or not injury is reasonably foreseeable to the pregnant woman such that the child might be born in an injured condition.

There has been a growing body of American and Commonwealth authority in favour of a remedy. Though some American[45] States have not been altogether happy about allowing recovery if the foetus (as in thalidomide cases) was not viable, that is, capable of independent life, at the time of injury, this limitation has rarely been applied in practice. The Law Commission in this country has conducted extensive research into the whole area, culminating in its 1974 Report which states: 'It is highly probable that the common law would, in appropriate circumstances, provide a remedy for a plaintiff suffering from a pre-natal injury caused by another's fault'.[46] The same report contained a draft Congenital Disabilities (Civil Liability) Bill aimed at resolving residual doubts, and a private member's Bill based on it has since become law.[47] A right of action then has been definitively established by legislation, though its precise form may be varied at some later date in the light of the findings of the Pearson Commission. The trend of the modern case law, professional and academic support and public sympathy generated by the thalidomide tragedy all combined to produce this result.

Probably then a right of action for thalidomide children existed at the time and if this had been the only obstacle in their way it could have been surmounted. Nevertheless, there was sufficient uncertainty to raise doubts, and for these to be reflected in terms of the 1968 settlement. Legislation was desirable, not just to remove the doubts, but in order to delimit the extent of any such right, by anticipating some of the problems it would raise. A detailed examination of them would take us beyond the scope of our immediate inquiry, but a few should be mentioned, if only to illustrate how the thalidomide tragedy has stimulated constructive inquiry in an area where there is likely to be a growing need for legal guidelines.

Should the right depend upon the child being born alive, or extend to a stillborn child's loss of expectation of life? Though several American cases have permitted such actions, at least if the foetus was viable when the injury occurred, the United Kingdom statute permits compensation for loss of expectation of life only if the child survives for forty-eight hours. However the whole notion of such compensation, more particularly when it accrues to the deceased's estate, is currently under attack. It would seem more sensible to make the award part of a parental claim.

Should the unborn child be entitled subsequently to sue its mother for negligence during her pre-natal régime? Originally the Law Commission favoured such liability. Consultation with outside bodies led it to reverse this view as inappropriate, and the Act precludes any such right, except in respect of injuries caused by the mother's negligent driving, when the child's claim would be covered by the insurance provisions of the Road Traffic Act 1972. As the Bar Council commented: '. . . in any system of law there are areas in which logic and principle ought to yield to social acceptability and natural sentiment and . . . this particular liability lies in such an area'.

Should the right of action cover cases of *pre-conception* injury, such as might be induced by radiation? Under the Act there can be liability of this kind unless the parent(s) knew of the risk at the time of the conception.

Perhaps the most far-reaching extension would be that ventilated in American courts, so far with a singular lack of success, namely an action by the child claiming damages for being born, the so-called suit for 'wrongful life'. Obviously, claims based on medically irresponsible intercourse, or illegitimate or otherwise disadvantaged birth, would exhibit all the unwelcome social and moral features of an action by a child against its parent. One could foresee highly emotive and subjective judgements being made about which types of physical, psychological or social deprivation could justify such a right, not to mention formidable difficulties in assessing damages.

For the moment legal analysis of these questions may seem academic. But it would be unduly optimistic to assume that we shall never see a comparable drug disaster, whereas we may expect increasingly sophisticated techniques for keeping alive children who have suffered ante-natal injury.

A mother's claim against the manufacturer

It is a gruesome paradox, that far from suffering harm as an immediate consequence of taking thalidomide, the mother herself derived a benefit, in so far as it was effective both as a sedative and to counteract nausea and morning sickness. However, once it is acknowledged that the drug caused the deformed birth, there can be doubt that if negligence is established against the manufacturer she has a legitimate claim for compensation in respect of any recognisable psychiatric illness ('nervous shock'), pain and suffering and physical injury which she has *personally* sustained as a result of the birth, as well as special damages (that is, a sum to cover incidental losses particular to her case).

The original action in *S* v. *Distillers* (1969)[48] alleged negligence towards the mother as well as the child. As Mr Justice Hinchcliffe put it:

> So far as Mrs S's claim is concerned, it is plain that this lady suffered a grievous shock. For a happily married woman, it is difficult to comprehend any greater shock than seeing your child born mis-shapen and deformed. The fun and joy of motherhood is partially destroyed. Instead of enjoying and being able to show off the baby to your friends there is a natural reluctance to do so. This has not been the sort of shock which has worn off like so many cases of shock that come before the courts; this is permanent. Ever since the birth Mrs S has been depressed, anxious and worried. She is daily reminded of her handicap. There is always a cloud over her happiness. She now has to take drugs prescribed by her doctor and she has a sense of guilt which makes it harder for her to recover, although Heaven knows she has nothing to blame herself for. This unhappy lady is entitled to damages for grievous shock, for future travelling expenses quarterly, for special clothes for the boy, together with something for the loss of wages. I award this plaintiff the sum of £5,000.

In one respect a mother's claim is clearly stronger than that of the child, in that there is no problem of a possible lack of capacity to sue. This apart, the nature of the claim would be substantially the same — alleged negligence in marketing the drug. If the children could succeed in negligence, clearly the mothers could too.

Claims against the retail chemist?

From a purely legal standpoint, it seems clear that a chemist could not be held liable (under English law) to a thalidomide *child*. Apart from any skill required in making up prescriptions, his function is essentially mechanical. He is not under a duty to carry out tests on the drugs which he dispenses, so that no question of negligence arises. Nor has he made a contract of any kind with the child.

The situation as between chemist and mother is more complicated. Again, the absence of negligence rules out any question of liability in tort, but is there any basis for a claim in contract? It would be very difficult to sustain if the drug was in fact obtained by the mothers only on prescription, because of the peculiar legal nature of the transaction.

In *Pfizer Corp.* v. *Ministry of Health* (1965)[49] the House of Lords held that the supply of drugs to a member of the public under the National Health Service Scheme, whether by a hospital or a pharmacist, was not a sale even though a prescription charge was paid. As Lord Reid put it:

> ... in my opinion there is no sale in this case. Sale is a consensual contract requiring agreement, express or implied. In the present case there appears to me to be no need for any agreement. The patient has a statutory right to demand the drug on payment of two shillings. The hospital has a statutory obligation to supply it on such payment. And if the prescription is presented to a chemist he appears to be bound by his contract with the appropriate authority to supply the drug on receipt of such payment. There is no need for any agreement between the patient and either the hospital or the chemist, and there is certainly no room for bargaining.

This case concerned drugs obtained by an out-patient at a hospital dispensary, but the same point was made explicitly with reference to supply by a chemist by the Lord Chief Justice, Lord Parker, in *Appleby* v. *Sleep* (1968)[50]: 'The first thing that is clear is that there will have been no sale by the chemist to the patient ...'.

Since the transaction is not a sale, it would not at first sight seem possible to invoke the provisions of the Sale of Goods Act 1893 (as amended), which, as we shall see, impose a strict liability on the seller of defective goods which cause injury. It has however been suggested by Atiyah that: 'It would ... be a mistake to conclude that the patient would necessarily be remediless in such circumstances if defective drugs were supplied, even in the absence of negligence'.[51] His argument is based on the approach of the House of Lords in *Young and Marten Ltd.* v. *McManus Childs Ltd.* (1969),[52] where, though the contract was one for the supply of labour and materials and therefore not technically a sale of *goods*, the court was prepared to hold that the supplier owed the same obligations as to the implied quality of his materials as if the transaction had been covered by the Act. Because the Act merely reaffirmed established common law principles in respect of those contracts to which it did apply it was seen as artificial not to apply the same criteria to a substantially similar transaction: '... the larger the element of supply of particular goods in the contract, the closer should be the similarity of warranties to be implied with those arising on a sale'.[53]

The difficulty remains that the above case clearly envisages the existence of a *contract* of some kind, and the fact that there is a statutory *entitlement* to prescription drugs would seem to rule out not only sale but any notion of contractual obligation at all as between chemist and patient. But aside from this admittedly formidable obstacle, the transaction closely resembles a contract. The element of 'supply of particular goods' is obviously a major characteristic of it. In so far as the chemist has a personal responsibility to make up the prescription one might reasonably expect even more onerous obligations on him than are required of an ordinary retailer. And it would seem invidious to distinguish between the provision of prescription drugs and sales of other drugs over the counter, especially as many drugs may be obtained in either way, as was initially the case with thalidomide.

What would the legal position have been in respect of a deformed birth resulting from thalidomide sold over the counter, or if the analogy with sale were accepted? The Sale of Goods Act 1893 (as amended)[54] requires that the seller's goods should be of merchantable quality. We can discount the narrow, even perverse, argument that thalidomide satisfied this requirement simply because it did act effectively, even for pregnant women, in that it was beneficial for *them*. A drug which had such disastrous secondary consequences was patently not of merchantable quality as far as they were concerned. But it might be objected that, by virtue of their condition, they constituted a very limited and special category of customer. Should the relevant criterion be the adequacy of the drug as a sedative for people in general?

The case law on this subject is of considerable complexity, but it is submitted that there are strong grounds for believing that the chemist would be held liable. Judicial and statutory interpretations of 'merchantability'[55] amount to little more than the proposition that the goods must be as fit for the purposes for which such goods are commonly bought as it is reasonable to expect, having regard to all the circumstances of the case. A drug which a doctor could reasonably prescribe for a pregnant woman's nausea or morning sickness, but which produced deformed births, could hardly be described as 'merchantable'. It should be emphasised that in contract the seller's inability to know or discover that the product is defective is irrelevant.

In the unlikely event of such a drug being deemed merchantable, another possibly relevant requirement of the Sale of Goods Act is that goods must be reasonably fit for any particular purpose made known by the buyer.[56] In the event of a woman in early pregnancy having identified the purpose for which she wanted the drug, it seems that the chemist would not have been able to argue that thalidomide was 'reasonably' fit for its purpose as a sedative if it was innocuous for the vast majority of its users. In this regard a dictum of Lord Pearce in *Kendall* v.

Lillico (1969)[57] is most instructive:

> I would expect a tribunal of fact to decide that a car sold in this country was reasonably fit for touring even though it was not well adapted for conditions in a heat-wave: but not, if it could not cope adequately with rain. If, however, it developed some lethal or dangerous trick in very hot weather, I would expect it to be found unfit. *In deciding the question of fact the rarity of the unsuitability would be weighed against the gravity of its consequences.*

This affords a striking parallel in the realm of contract with the negligence principle that gravity of risk may in appropriate circumstances be the overriding criterion of liability.

Claims against the doctor?

Doctors have always jealously guarded their independence in matters of prescribing. When, for example, in 1955, the Government tried to impose a total ban on the use of heroin in medical practice, its failure was largely due to the opposition of the medical profession which saw the proposal as an interference with their freedom of decision. Similar objections were voiced in 1968, when the right to prescribe heroin was limited to doctors in special treatment centres.

Of all the people involved in the process by which a patient ends up taking a drug – from the manufacturer, through the licensing authority, to the doctor and the pharmacist – it is the doctor who is the most immediately instrumental in the choice of the particular drug which is taken. It is on the exercise of his proclaimed independent judgement that the patient ultimately relies, and he relies to a much greater extent on this 'seller' than does the shopper at the supermarket.

One can see the temptation to argue that a necessary corollary of that independence is a corresponding liability in negligence when things go wrong. But while this is true of careless diagnosis or treatment, it would be unreal to impose it in respect of routine prescribing. More particularly, in the context of present-day medical practice the 'reasonable' doctor cannot be expected, any more than the chemist, to analyse the drugs which he prescribes, and it is submitted that on that ground alone an attempt to establish negligence on his part merely for having prescribed thalidomide would be bound to fail.

Claims against the licensing authority?

If the manufacturer of a defective drug can be held liable in negligence, is there not a case for imposing liability also on the governmental authority which licenses it? When this question was posed in the House of Commons debate on thalidomide in November 1972, Sir Keith Joseph replied:

> I must state clearly that compensation is not for the Government to provide. There is no legal liability on the Government. There is no legal implication about a drug because it was prescribed under the National Health Service. There was no scrutiny system until the Committee on the Safety of Drugs was set up as a result of the thalidomide tragedy. Compensation is a matter for the company.[58]

When asked if the Government would be responsible now that the Medicines Commission had been set up, he added: 'It is still the responsibility of the manufacturer to answer for his manufacture, whether there is a scrutiny system or not. By a scrutiny system we provide the public with as much protection as we can, but the responsibility is still upon the manufacturer'.[59]

Should a government seal of approval import a measure of financial responsibility? At this stage we need only note the position when thalidomide was marketed. At that time, 'dangerous drugs' and certain 'biological' products apart, there was no restriction on a drug manufacturer's right to put any new product on the market. The only form of official supervision was by the Standing Joint Committee on the Classification of Proprietary Medicines (the Cohen Committee) which attempted to categorise the effectiveness and safety of drugs and was entitled to indicate that adequate clinical trials had not been carried out. It allocated thalidomide to Category 'N', for drugs of proved therapeutic value, implying that all the expected tests had been carried out.

In one sense the Government's immunity from liability was a corollary of the doctor's independent right to prescribe. Unlike the doctor (or the manufacturer) it is not concerned to influence the public to take a particular drug, or to tell doctors which drugs they should prescribe. It was the responsibility of the Minister of Health to see that a service was available to patients. Putting the point another way, there was, for legal purposes, an insufficient causal link between the Standing Committee's classification and a patient's decision to take thalidomide to establish liability on the part of the Government.

47

Judicial assessment of damages

In the original settlement in *S* v. *Distillers* (1968) the child in the most serious injury range was awarded £52,000. (less 60 per cent). The expert actuary called on his behalf estimated his loss at £135,000. The child in the middle range received £32,000 (less 60 per cent). The actuary's assessment was £78,500. How are such wide disparities possible? What methods do the courts use in calculating damages and, in particular, what does the judge's approach in *S* v. *Distillers* tell us about the adequacy of those methods in general?

The whole area of assessment of damages for personal injuries is beset by intractable, ultimately unanswerable, questions. The root problem is that since money and injury are incommensurables there can be no truly satisfactory criteria for evaluating such loss in financial terms, except, that is, for items such as wages lost before trial and medical expenses incurred. Some Socialist legal systems have drawn the seemingly harsh conclusion that it is undesirable to make any award of damages at all for non-material loss, a solution which reflects priorities in the allocation of resources as well, perhaps, as distaste for reducing human suffering to monetary terms. When injuries are as severe and emotive as in the case of thalidomide this sense of the inappropriateness of a financial solution is easy enough to understand. But much of its force rests upon the false premise that the money is designed, as it were, to blot out the injury, rather than to provide compensation which is often sorely needed. If then one grants the desirability in principle of compensation for non-material loss, there remains the problem of finding criteria by which to evaluate it.

The dilemma is neatly expressed by Ogus in the phrase 'a foot, a feeling or a function'.[60] In other words, are such damages to be awarded on a tariff basis, or for loss of happiness, or as solace for the loss of function attributable to the injury? Nor is it only compensation for the injury itself which is problematic. Equally difficult in a case such as thalidomide is the assessment of loss of future earnings. It is worth recalling that it was precisely the failure of the parties to agree on the amount of damages which led to the court having to decide the matter; though it should also be noted that even where the parties reach agreement by themselves, the law requires a settlement on behalf of children to receive court approval.

The various heads under which damages may be claimed at common law are easy enough to state. A distinction is drawn between pecuniary and non-pecuniary loss. Pecuniary loss comprises loss of earnings and earning capacity, as well as all past and future medical expenditure reasonably incurred as a result of the injury. Non-pecuniary loss covers pain and suffering, loss of expectation of life, and loss of amenities (the reduced capacity to enjoy life resulting from loss of limbs or faculties).

The award is made in the form of a lump sum, on a once-for-all basis, so that subsequent events, such as radical deterioration or, for that matter, improvement in the plaintiff's condition are to be ignored. Until recently it was also the usual practice for judges to make global awards without necessarily specifying the amounts attributable to particular heads of damage. Since the Administration of Justice Act 1969, as interpreted in *Jefford* v. *Gee* (1970),[61] some degree of itemisation is now required because there are different interest rates applicable to pre-trial pecuniary and non-pecuniary loss. But the component parts, the heads of damages within these categories, still need not be itemised. One clear merit of even more itemisation is that it would lead to more predictability and thus facilitate settlements out of court.

It is obvious that the criteria of assessment are inescapably arbitrary in so far as one cannot meaningfully price human life or differentiate, except within broad limits, between the value of individual limbs and their functioning. But relative uniformity of awards is desirable, both to provide equality of treatment in comparable cases and to facilitate settlements. Now that in England damages are almost invariably assessed by judges, a degree of consistency has been achieved, by building on previous decisions to establish conventional sums for particular kinds of injury, while bearing in mind individual differences such as age, occupation and leisure pursuits and making adjustments to the tariffs from time to time to reflect the fall in the value of money.

In *S* v. *Distillers*, the unique features of the case made what is always an unenviable task immeasurably harder. As Mr Justice Hinchcliffe commented:

> Never can there have been two cases where there are so many imponderable factors. It is fair to say that the court is asked to speculate upon every aspect of damage. If ever there was a case where a broad view should be taken as to what is just and reasonable compensation, this is it.[62]

Pecuniary loss

Let us first consider the judge's approach to pecuniary loss — that is loss of earnings and medical expenses of various kinds. The assessment of medical expenses need not detain us other than to note that the novelty of the injuries made anticipated future needs more speculative than is normally the case. Much more significant in determining the overall

49

amounts awarded were the judge's attitude to actuarial evidence and his approach to inflation.

In several passages of the judgement he expresses distinct reservations about the value of actuarial evidence, culminating in these observations:

> I very much regret that I have taken up so much time in dealing with the question of the actuarial evidence and how it should be regarded, but it is not my fault ... I get the impression that the reformers would like an alteration in the law so that in assessing damages pecuniary loss would be itemised and based on actuarial consideration. That time has not yet arrived.[63]

We have just seen that a start has been made in the process of itemisation. It is equally to be hoped that much more reliance will be placed on actuarial aids in the future. Nor is this a vain hope, since the 'reformers' include the Law Commission, which has been pressing for more extensive use of actuarial expertise for several years and in 1973 advocated legislation to facilitate it.[64]

Judicial reluctance to rely on actuarial evidence seems to be compounded of a variety of objections, few of which seem tenable. It is all the more disquieting when one considers that the courts seem to have been more flexible on the matter in the late nineteenth century in England and that today such evidence is used almost as a matter of course in a number of American and Commonwealth jurisdictions. John Prevett, the expert actuary called for the plaintiffs in *S* v. *Distillers*, has described this judicial aversion as reflecting a lack of communication between the two professions.[65] Some judges have explained their attitude as stemming from a fear that the mechanical application of tables would give an illusion of accuracy, while failing to take account of the chance occurrences of life, with the result that awards would normally be inflated. Mr Justice Hinchcliffe expressly adopted the words of one of the judges in an Australian case: 'that a preoccupation with actuarial figures led the jury [in England it would be a judge] to a lop-sided view of the case, with the result that they failed in their overriding duty to be fair to both parties'.[66] A variant of this criticism is that actuarial tables deal with averages, whereas the courts are concerned with individuals. But it seems clear enough that this kind of criticism is misconceived precisely because it presupposes a mechanical application of actuarial evidence, instead of regarding it as a framework establishing norms to be applied or varied in the particular circumstances of the case.

A more plausible fear is that of disproportionately increased expense and delay if conflicting actuarial evidence were to become a standard feature of accident cases. The Law Commission is investigating the feasibility of a court actuarial service, or standard actuarial tables to cover the vast majority of cases.

It is hard to avoid the conclusion that judicial resistance is, in part at least, explained by a traditional mistrust of any innovation which reduces the human element in legal proceedings — thereby encroaching on judicial autonomy — in favour of a mechanised or scientific approach. It is the same aversion which has resisted the tape recorder and will doubtless resist the computer. One could have more sympathy for such misgivings if the method which the judges do employ were not itself essentially an actuarial one, albeit of a primitive kind, despite their insistence on regarding it as a different form of assessment. Thus in calculating lost future earnings they estimate the amount by which the plaintiff's yearly earnings (or earning capacity) will have diminished as a result of the accident and multiply it by what is known as the 'multiplier', a figure *less* than the actual number of years he is expected to continue working, in order to take account of contingencies such as early death or retirement, illness, or unemployment and of the financial advantage of receiving an immediate lump sum. In practice the multiplier has rarely exceeded sixteen years, however young the plaintiff. It is thus bound to be somewhat arbitrary. Actuaries seldom deduct more than 5 per cent for contingencies.

If undue deduction for contingencies suggests that the level of awards may be too low, the judicial approach to inflation, especially in the light of recent economic trends, is an even greater cause for concern. Even in 1968 it was arguably the primary factor casting doubt on the adequacy of awards.

As Ogus has pointed out,[67] there are broadly four possible approaches to the problem of anticipated future inflation. First, there is the Draconian solution of totally ignoring its incidence as being too speculative to take account of. Secondly, one might accept the evidence of economists as expert witnesses, a course which has been strongly opposed by the courts. Thus Mr Justice Hinchcliffe took the view that '. . . the evidence of Professor Day, distinguished economist from the London School of Economics, was inadmissible since it was based on speculation and hearsay'.[68] The currently favoured view, endorsed in *S v. Distillers*, is that, while it is unrealistic simply to ignore inflation, loss due to it is balanced by the advantage of being able to invest the lump sum awarded. As Lord Diplock put it in *Mallett* v. *McMonagle*, in 1969:

Experience of the twenty years of inflation [up to 1969] has shown that its effects can be offset to some extent at any rate by prudent investment in buying a home, in growth stocks, or in the short term high-interest bearing securities.[69]

The same view seems to have been taken by the majority of the House of Lords in the leading case of *Taylor* v. *O'Connor*[70] in the following year. It is submitted that whatever plausibility this view had in the twenty years up to 1969, when the purchasing power of the pound fell by 3–3½ per cent per annum on average, in the last few years it has been exposed as untenable, most obviously so in mid-1975 with wage inflation running at 30 per cent. Moreover, it presupposes a degree of expertise, or continued access to it, and a perseverance which the average accident victim could hardly be blamed for not displaying. As Professor Street commented in an article written in September 1972:

> Consider, then, what the plaintiff is expected to do with the lump sum damages awarded to him. He has to invest them in shares, some of which he has to sell every few months to meet his needs; these shares must earn five per cent after tax (and he will have no earned income allowance) and be sold off at fixed times and yet at a price which, after allowing for capital gains tax, broker's commissions and the bought and sold price gap, give him an average capital profit to keep up with, say, a six per cent per annum compound rate of increase.[71]

We have here a classic example of how the law is prone to operate in a kind of social void, in an area where it could usefully benefit from sociological investigation, in this instance into the social consequences of lump sum awards. If the incidence of their dissipation is as serious as journalistic accounts of the decline and fall of pools winners would have us believe, there is a strong case for a more paternalistic approach, perhaps by enabling the court to order periodical payments, as is possible in several continental and Socialist systems. On the other hand, where large sums of money are at stake litigants will normally have received advice on investments, at least initially.

At all events, in the most recent case on this issue, *Young* v. *Percival*,[72] in 1974, the Court of Appeal reaffirmed the established principle and applied *Taylor* v. *O'Connor*. It is true that they added: 'We have indeed misgivings about the applicability of the decision in present-day conditions', but felt that in any event there was 'no firm or workable principle, or basis of calculation, to put in its place'. It is interesting that, almost as an afterthought, at the end of the judgement, the court observed:

> ... It might be argued that, if present day inflationary conditions are likely to continue, any successful attempt by the courts to protect plaintiffs in cases such as the present from the effects of such conditions would mean that such plaintiffs, rightly or wrongly, would be made into a specially favoured class as compared with the generality of the public.[73]

This seems a curious and suspect argument, at least as regards pecuniary loss, which is intended to put the plaintiff in the financial position he would have enjoyed but for the injury. It is hard to see why, in principle, he should not be protected against inflation in this respect. Nor, in practice, judging from past experience of the rate of wage inflation relative to the rate of price inflation, would he in fact enjoy a privileged position. How best to take account of inflation remains something of a problem. But the Law Commission has expressed optimism about the feasibility of actuarial tables including a variable factor for it, based on economists' predictions.

The fourth possible approach identified by Ogus is to abandon lump sum awards and to adopt a periodical payment system which, if geared to a cost-of-living index, would virtually dispose of the difficulty, as well as facilitate adjustment to other changing circumstances, such as a change in the victim's condition or alterations in tax laws. There would be nothing radical in such a measure. We already have this system for social security benefits and it is the normal method of payment for divorce maintenance. The main obstacle is said to be that no one concerned appears to want it in personal injuries litigation. As the Law Commission discovered: 'Consultation has left us in no doubt that the introduction of a system of periodic payments would meet with vehement opposition from almost every person or organisation actually concerned with personal injury litigation'.[74] Insurance companies do not relish the prospect of protracted administration in an already unprofitable field; trade unions prize the opportunity to negotiate for a lump sum as an inducement to membership. However, it could be argued that taxpayers and premium payers in general are 'concerned', if the practical consequence of dissipating a lump sum is recourse to public funds.

It should be emphasised that the discussion in this chapter has been confined to possible improvements within the existing structure of common law fault liability. Periodical payments would be more easily accommodated in an administrative system akin to that in force for industrial injuries benefit, and this approach will be considered in chapter 5.

Non-pecuniary loss

Moving to the question of non-material loss, where it is immediately apparent that we are in the realms of the unknowable, it is not surprising that the judges have fallen back on a tariff system, varied in individual cases to take account of special characteristics. In the case of thalidomide children the medical evidence established that there was no loss of expectation of life, so that we are concerned exclusively with damages for pain and suffering and loss of amenity.

Damages are awarded when there is 'clear evidence of reasonably prolonged suffering' due to the injury itself and any consequential treatment. They may include a sum for the mental anguish of knowing that one's capacity to enjoy life has been diminished by physical handicap: 'each child when not asleep is fully aware that he is not like others and cannot behave like a normal child'.[75] One justification for standardised awards under this head is that it would be invidious to draw distinctions on the basis of differential pain thresholds. As Lord Pearce said in *West* v. *Shephard* (1964)[76] : 'It would be lamentable if the trial of a personal injury claim put a premium on protestations of misery and if a long face was the only safe passport to a large reward'.

For similar reasons, the courts have generally adopted an essentially objective view of the claim for loss of amenity. This is most graphically demonstrated in *West* v. *Shephard*, where a majority of the House of Lords took the view that a permanently unconscious plaintiff was entitled to substantial damages for his deprivation. But a strong body of judicial opinion favours a subjective approach to loss of amenity, either by equating it with loss of happiness, or as entitling the victim to compensation as solace for his condition, and thus relating it to his degree of awareness and appreciation of that condition.

Though he is not very explicit about his approach, Mr Justice Hinchcliffe seems to have opted for a subjective analysis, taking 'a broad view'. Perhaps this was inevitable where there were 'no awards in comparable cases to guide the court'. Not only was there no existing tariff for thalidomide injuries, but because these were cases of ante-natal injury, even the conventional vocabulary of 'loss' of limbs and of amenities is inadequate:

> In the long run it is the court which takes into consideration all the circumstances of the case ... and then decides what is fair

54

compensation to both parties. The assessment of the global sum is based on experience and by the application of reasonable common sense . . .[77]

It will be noticed that the judge uses the phrase 'fair compensation *to both parties*', and says elsewhere that 'a fair and *moderate* value has to be placed on the disability and the consequential loss'. There is certainly nothing unusual in such sentiments; indeed in *Warren* v. *King* (1963)[78] the Court of Appeal held that a failure to warn a jury about the need for moderation and fairness *to the defendant* in assessing damages constituted a misdirection. What is interesting about this criterion is not only that it involves a consideration which is never clarified and is wholly extrinsic to the main rationales of compensation – a tariff basis, loss of happiness, or solace – but that it illustrates the refusal of the courts to attach significance to whether or not the defendant is insured.

We are not suggesting that 'anything goes' by way of damages where insurance companies are the effective defendants. Naturally regard must be had to the total cost of insurance premiums. But if the level of damages in personal injury cases has been kept low by a supposed need to be 'fair' to the defendant, this emphasises the artificiality of a system wedded to fault liability, nominally rooted in a one-to-one confrontation between the parties, but increasingly operating in an economic background of insurance based on risk, with every expectation that disputes will never reach the courts.

The role of insurance

Orthodox legal theory maintains, then, that the existence or absence of insurance has to be ignored when the court is resolving the issues of liability and damages as between the parties. The law of negligence is concerned with *shifting* the loss from plaintiff to defendant when the latter is shown to be at fault. The mechanism of insurance on the other hand serves to *distribute* losses and spread the risk of injury. This is not to say that the existence of insurance has had no impact on the law. The tension between the legal theory of loss-shifting and the economic reality of loss-spreading is a paradox which lies at the heart of the present system, and is reflected in the case law in various ways. But the judges have drawn back from relinquishing the fault requirement or themselves widening the ambit of liability, partly because it would falsify the basis on which existing insurance policies have been negotiated. Stricter liability would obviously lead to an increase in premiums. Any such change is therefore only likely to come about through legislation, as Lord Wilberforce indicated in *Morgans* v. *Launchbury* (1972).[79]

Yet despite the apparent judicial adherence to 'fault', we have seen that the standard of care demanded of manufacturers, among others, has been raised over the years and plainly this process and the general level of damages awarded have been influenced by insurance. As Lord Denning observed in *Morris* v. *Ford Motor Co. Ltd.* (1973)[80] — a case involving injury to a worker:

> The damages are expected to be borne by the insurers. The courts themselves recognise this every day. They would not find negligence so readily — or award sums of such increasing magnitude — except on the footing that the damages are to be borne . . . by an insurance company.

In recent years judges have been more explicitly concerned as to how the law might adapt to the economic realities. In *Spartan Steel and Alloys Ltd.* v. *Martin and Co. (Contractors) Ltd.* (1972),[81] Lord Denning, a forthright proponent of this approach, expressly utilised a risk distribution analysis in reaching his decision.

Since insurance companies usually have effective control over the conduct of negotiations on behalf of defendants, and only a minute proportion of cases reach the stage of a court hearing, it is necessary to consider more closely the effect of a defendant's contract of insurance on the outcome.[82]

It is standard practice for a manufacturer to insure against the risk of negligence liability. The insurers undertake to indemnify him, up to an agreed amount, in respect of his legal liability to pay compensation for injury to users of his products. The precise legal implications of the contract of insurance will always depend on the particular terms of the policy. In the pharmaceutical industry, for example, it is not uncommon for design defects to be specifically excluded from cover. Typically a policy will include all types of goods supplied by the insured, though in the case of pharmaceutical products it may be limited to specified items. Products liability insurance often contains a periodic limit, usually in the form of an aggregate amount for a given year. But when liability is limited to 'any one event', as it was in Distillers' contract with their insurers, it may be unclear whether this means a given amount in respect of each individual case, or a sum to cover all cases relating to the period in question.

The policy normally gives the insurers the right to exercise full control over the negotiations and decide on what terms, if any, a settlement is acceptable to them. They will be entitled to conduct such negotiations in the defendant's name, often requiring him to deal with claimants in accordance with their instructions, while they remain in the background. If the insured fails to comply and prejudices the insurer's position by admitting liability or negotiating a settlement independently, the insurers are released from liability. Of course, a company facing adverse publicity, anxious to preserve its goodwill and under strong pressure from its institutional investors, may look to its insurers to settle where legal liability is doubtful. But the decision remains that of the insurers.

In the absence of knowledge of the terms of Distillers' contract of insurance with a syndicate of Lloyds underwriters, some of the comment on the thalidomide negotiations has been reminiscent of *Hamlet* without the prince. At the time of writing, Distillers are suing the insurers, who have disclaimed liability on grounds of non-disclosure of relevant facts and failure to carry out adequate tests and research on the drug. Though we are unable to comment on this particular action, what has been said about the importance of insurance in personal injury litigation prompts consideration of the procedure for settlements. For what must ultimately concern us is the adequacy of legal processes to cope with accident cases generally.

The settlement process

English civil procedure purports to be a series of steps delimiting and clarifying the issues between the parties with a view to resolving their dispute at a trial. In reality, largely because the parties prepare their own cases with virtually no official supervision, the process serves to conceal as much as it reveals. But in any event the overwhelming majority of personal injury actions are settled out of court. The elaborate rules of procedure are in the main designed for an eventuality which seldom occurs.

The thalidomide litigation was never put to the test of a court decision on the merits, but, because it was a settlement of infants' claims, certain special legal considerations applied. Whereas in English law an agreement between adults to settle a legal dispute is treated as a binding contract, this is not the case with infants. They normally remain at liberty to reject the terms of a settlement, even where it proved acceptable to their legal representative or 'next friend'. The Rules of the Supreme Court therefore expressly provide that once proceedings have been initiated on behalf of an infant, a settlement, to be legally binding, requires the approval of the court, as in the initial settlement in *S.* v. *Distillers*. In exercising its discretion whether or not to approve, the court will have to consider the adequacy of the amount offered and the likelihood of the infant succeeding had the case been fought. Commenting in a case in November 1972 on the outcome of *S.* v. *Distillers*, the Lord Chief Justice, Lord Widgery, observed: 'Whether this was a sensible and suitable settlement on behalf of the children is not for us to say, but we see no reason on the information before us to think that it was other than a sensible conclusion in the face of all the difficulties which lay in the children's path'.[83]

Approximately 95 per cent of all personal injury claims are settled. Those that are not may take three years or so before they are heard, if the amounts involved are substantial and the case has to be decided in the High Court. It is therefore obvious that if all cases were fully litigated there would be delays of such Dickensian proportions that the whole legal process would simply grind to a halt. Settlements represent the bulk of conflict resolution in the tort system and it is necessary to examine the forces at work in this bargaining process, which is in turn influenced by the way the rules of civil procedure operate in practice. For the terms on which a party is prepared to settle are dictated in part by his assessment of the strength of his case. Only if he can elicit certain relevant information from the other side will he be able to make a meaningful assessment.

We have no wish to decry the extensive use of settlements. In principle the resolution of legal conflict without the parties having to go to court is socially desirable, as well as administratively unavoidable. It is in the public interest in that a large proportion of civil litigation attracts legal aid paid out of general taxation. A settlement can be a victory for common sense and reasonableness, whereas an impending court action can engender much bitterness. 'Litigation neurosis' is a not infrequent accompaniment of emotionally fraught cases, and is arguably accentuated in an adversary system such as ours where law-suits — particularly in the higher courts — have all the characteristics of a battle between the parties, in which the judge does not descend into the arena to take on the role of investigator, still less that of conciliator.

In the County Court the judge may assume a more investigatory role and in many types of tribunal the procedure lends itself to conciliation. Recently there has been a marked shift towards more use of mediation and arbitration techniques in the resolution of disputes, as witness the introduction of a small claims arbitration procedure in the County Court and the emphasis on conciliation in areas such as industrial relations, race relations and sex discrimination. But the thalidomide actions had to be dealt with at High Court level, where the gladiatorial approach to litigation is most pronounced.

In principle then settlements are to be encouraged and legal advisers will normally recommend their clients to settle in accident cases. But the rules of procedure, geared to the possibility of an eventual confrontation in court, provide relatively few positive aids to settlement. Instead they consist of elaborate preparatory stages which supposedly 'clear the decks' for the (usually non-existent) trial. Despite rules which pay formal lip-service to a policy of 'cards on the table', in practice each side typically proceeds with the minimum of disclosure required. As a *Justice* report has put it: 'Pleading . . . resembles nothing so much as naval warfare before the advent of radar, when each side made blind forays into the sea area of the other, while giving away as little as possible about the disposition of his own forces'.[84]

The very intricacy of the procedure gives an advantage to the party who can best afford both the time and money to exploit the rules to the full. This is not to say that the rules of procedure totally disregard the likelihood that the parties will settle. The moment litigation is pending or contemplated, negotiations may proceed on a 'without prejudice' footing, so that communications between the parties, including offers of settlement, become privileged and cannot be relied on as admissions if no agreement is reached. Also, if a defendant makes an offer of settlement by way of 'payment into court', the plaintiff will have to pay all the costs subsequently incurred if he refuses the offer, continues the action and is awarded less than the amount paid in. Since the costs of the trial represent the bulk of the total costs, he is often well-advised to accept.

One rule as to costs provides a powerful incentive for parties to settle in most actions. Though the normal order made by the judge is that the loser pays the winner's costs as well as his own, this will not in practice cover the whole of the winner's expenditure. It is only his reasonably necessary or 'proper' costs that the loser must pay, that is those *necessarily* incurred after the writ has been issued. But prudent preparation of a case will involve more expenditure than this and successful litigants frequently have to pay anything up to a third of their total costs themselves, and may still face the prospect of losing on appeal. This is quite apart from the risk of losing in the first place, which on any reasonable view meant a real danger of financial disaster for thalidomide families. When one father told a solicitor from Kimber, Bull that if necessary he would pursue the case on his own, he was reputedly told that it could cost him £250,000!

It is true that many thalidomide parents satisfied the means test for legal aid and that the action which formed the basis of the initial settlement was legally aided. However, an applicant who is eligible financially must first show that he has reasonable grounds for bringing proceedings and they may still be refused legal aid, 'if it appears unreasonable that he should receive it in the particular circumstances of the case'.[85] This second test covers situations where there is an arguable case in law, but it would not be reasonable to pursue it. Since public funds are at stake, the standard criterion is whether or not a sensible and prudent paying client would be advised to spend his own money on the case. Once the £3¼ million offer had been made, it is by no means certain that legal aid to fight the case to a conclusion would have been forthcoming.

The paradox of a system geared to the possibility of trial while conceding the reality of settlement has many ramifications. For example, the knowledge that a trial is unlikely is a disincentive to building up costs by requesting detailed particulars of the opposing side's case. But an inevitable consequence is that it is that much more difficult to find out the true strength of your own case, in order to know on what terms an acceptable settlement can be reached.

Granted that settlements are desirable, one must be wary of being impressed by their sheer volume, as distinct from their adequacy or fairness. We have just seen that the standard rule as to costs is a feature of the legal system itself which frequently compels settlement on unfavourable terms. Bearing in mind that parties seek advantageous settlements rather than fair ones anyway, what are the pressures from outside the legal system which dictate the outcome in personal injury cases?

It should be evident from our account of the case history in chapter 1 that the low income plaintiff fighting a large company in an accident case presents a paradigm of cards being stacked against the plaintiff. The whole settlement machinery gives a built-in advantage to the defendant company, with its well-staffed legal division and its financial interest (and that of its insurance company) in delay, so that even if money has ultimately to be paid it remains available for investment in the meantime. For the plaintiff the exact converse holds true. And not only does he normally need the money as soon as possible, but the prospect of litigation – perhaps a once-in-a-lifetime event – may evoke in him a degree of fear and suspicion barely comprehensible to an institutional defendant which regards it as a routine aspect of its work.

While it may be true that in the thalidomide litigation neither side wanted to go to *court*, and the negotiations had an air of 'shadow-boxing' about them, nonetheless the plaintiffs needed to 'fight' in order to obtain an adequate settlement. The initial insistence by the defendants on 100 per cent acceptance of the £3¼ million offer, coupled with the 'pressurising' of the dissentients at the public meetings, constituted an extreme version of an all too familiar situation. Where the thalidomide story differed was in the effectiveness of the public campaign as momentum built up in the media and Parliament, so that the plaintiffs emerged as an identifiable and relatively cohesive force with strong public support, ultimately strong enough to convince institutional investors to exercise their influence in a wholly uncharacteristic way.

Notes

[1] [1932] A.C.562, 580.

[2] [1970] A.C.1004, 1027.

[3] The classic example was the doctrine of 'common employment', under which an employer was not deemed responsible for torts committed by one of his employees on a fellow employee.

[4] [1964] A.C.465, 536, italics supplied.

[5] [1932] A.C.562.

[6] For example, *Grant* v. *Australian Knitting Mills* [1936] A.C.85; *Mason* v. *Williams and Williams*, [1955] 1 All E.R.808.

[7] Tony Weir, *A Casebook on Tort*, Sweet and Maxwell (3rd ed.), 1974, p. 21.

[8] See p. 31

[9] [1975] 1 All E.R.41, 51.

[10] See *Donoghue* v. *Stevenson* [1932] A.C.562, 598 *per* Lord Atkin; and 617–18 *per* Lord MacMillan.

[11] D.W. Greig, *Sale of Goods*, Butterworths 1974, p. 254.

[12] Many American decisions have held the manufacturer of the end product responsible for negligence by anyone in the production process. See, e.g., *Ford Motor Co.* v. *Mathis* (1963), 322 F.2d 267. Cf. *Second Restatement of Torts*, s.400; and Draft European Convention on Products Liability in regard to Personal Injury and Death (1975), Art. 3(2).

In English law, the manufacturer of the completed product will probably escape liability for the supplier's negligence by showing that he has taken all reasonable care in the selection and, where appropriate, supervision of the supplier: *Taylor* v. *Rover Co.* [1966] 2 All E.R.181.

[13] Cf. *Roe* v. *Minister of Health* [1954] 2 Q.B.66, 92 *per* Morris, L.J.: 'Care has to be exercised to ensure that conduct in 1947 is only judged in the light of knowledge which then was or ought reasonably to have been possessed. In this connexion the then-existing state of medical literature must be had in mind.'

[14] *Barnett* v. *Chelsea and Kensington Hospital Management Committee* [1969] 1 Q.B.428.

[15] B. Brodie, 'Idiosyncracy and Intolerance', in G. Wolstenholme and R. Porter, (eds), *Drug Responses in Man*, Churchill 1967.

[16] H. Marshall Taylor, quoted in *Thalidomide and the Power of the Drug Companies*, pp. 169–70.

[17] D. Woollam, 'The Thalidomide Disaster Considered as an Experiment in Mammalian Teratology', *British Medical Journal*, vol. 2, 1962, pp. 236–7.

[18] D. Woollam, letter to *British Medical Journal*, vol. 2, 1962, p. 406.

[19] E. Lesser, 'Thalidomide and the Pharmacologists', *New Scientist*, 23 May 1974, p. 473.

[20] *Thalidomide and the Power of the Drug Companies*, p. 187.

[21] See J. Lear, 'The Unfinished Story of Thalidomide', *Saturday Review*, 1 September 1962, pp. 36–7.

[22] [1954] 2 Q.B.66, 84.

[23] Cf. *Paris* v. *Stepney Borough Council* [1951] A.C.367.

[24] [1965] A.C.778.

[25] See H. Street, *The Law of Torts*, Butterworths (6th ed.), 1976, pp. 138–41.

[26] See cases cited in note 6.

[27] *Turner* v. *Mansfield Corporation, The Times* 15 May 1975, C.A.

[28] *Hedley Byrne and Co.* v. *Heller and Partners Ltd.* [1964] A.C.465.

[29] J.G. Fleming, *The Law of Torts*, The Law Book Co. Ltd. (4th ed.), 1971, p. 162, italics supplied.

[30] [1971] A.C.458.

[31] Common Law Procedure Act of New South Wales, No. 21 of 1899, s. 8(4) (as amended).

[32] See [1971] A.C.458, 466.

[33] Ibid., p. 469.

[34] W.H.V. Rogers, Winfield and Jolowicz on *Tort*, Sweet and Maxwell (10th ed.), 1975, p. 225.

[35] *Watson* v. *Buckley* [1940] 1 All E.R.174.

[36] Ibid., pp. 181, 183.

[37] For example, *Stevens* v. *Parke, Davis and Co.* (1973), 9 Cal. 3d 51, 58; *Love* v. *Wolf* (1964), 226 Cal. App. 2d 378.

[38] See *Wright* v. *Carter Products* (1957), 244 F.2d 53, 59.

[39] *Villar* v. *Gilbey* [1907] A.C.139, 144.

[40] *The George and Richard* (1871) L.R.3 Ad. and E.466.

[41] (1963) (2) S.A.254 (W), 259.

[42] (1884) 138 Mass. 14.

[43] (1891) L.R.Ir. 69.

[44] [1972] V.R.353.

[45 See *White* v. *Yup* (1969) 458 P.2d 617, 620–1. In *Jorgensen* v. *Meade Johnson* (1973), 483 F.2d 237, an action was brought against a pharmaceutical company on behalf of deceased and living mongoloid twins, alleging that their condition resulted from the mother taking a birth control pill manufactured by the company. An Oklahoma Court of Appeals held that such a claim disclosed a cause of action in principle, in negligence, strict tort liability, or warranty.

[46] The Law Commission, *Report on Injuries to Unborn Children*, 1974, Cmnd. 5709, p. 3.

[47] Congenital Disabilities (Civil Liability) Act 1976.

[48] [1969] 3 All E.R.1412, 1422.

[49] [1965] A.C.512, 535–6.

[50] [1968] 2 All E.R.265, 269.

[51] P.S. Atiyah, *The Sale of Goods*, Pitman (5th ed.), 1975, p. 5.

[52] [1969] 1 A.C.454.

[53] Ibid., p. 476, *per* Lord Wilberforce.

[54] By the Supply of Goods (Implied Terms) Act 1973.

[55] See now Sale of Goods Act 1893, s.14(2) and s.62(1A).

[56] Ibid., s.14(3) (as amended).

[57] [1969] 2 A.C.31, at p. 115, italics supplied.

[58] H.C. Deb., vol. 847, no. 22, col. 440–1, 29 November 1972.

[59] Ibid., col. 441.

[60] A.I. Ogus, 'Damages for Lost Amenities: for a Foot, a Feeling or a Function?' *Modern Law Review*, vol. 35, 1972, p. 1.

[61] [1970] 2 Q.B. 130.

[62] *S* v. *Distillers* [1969] 3 All E.R. 1412, 1422.

[63] Ibid., p. 1421.

[64] The Law Commission, *Report on Personal Injury Litigation – Assessment of Damages*, HMSO 1973, pp. 59–63.

[65] J.H. Prevett, 'Actuarial Assessment of Damages: The Thalidomide Case – 1', *Modern Law Review*, vol. 35, 1972, p. 140, at 141. See also p. 257.

[66] [1969] 3 All E.R.1412, 1420.

[67] A.I. Ogus, *The Law of Damages*, Butterworths 1973, pp. 192–3.

[68] [1969] 3 All E.R.1412, 1421.

[69] [1970] A.C.166, 175.

[70] [1971] A.C.115.

[71] *The Sunday Times*, 1 October 1972.

[72] *Young* v. *Percival* [1974] 3 All E.R.677.

[73] Ibid., at p. 688.

[74] *Report on Personal Injury Litigation*, op. cit., p. 10.

[75] [1969] 3 All E.R.1412, 1419.

[76] [1964] A.C.326, 368—9.

[77] [1969] 3 All E.R.1412, 1419.

[78] [1963] 3 All E.R.521.

[79] [1973] A.C.127.

[80] [1973] 1 Q.B. 792, 798.

[81] [1973] 1 Q.B. 27.

[82] See E.A. Heppell, *Products Liability Insurance*, Pitman 1967:

[83] *Attorney-General* v. *Times Newspapers Ltd.* [1972] 3 All E.R.1136, 1139.

[84] Justice, *Going to Law: A Critique of English Civil Procedure*, Stevens and Sons 1974, p. 13.

[85] See now Legal Aid Act 1974, s.7(5).

3 The legal issues:2 contempt of court and freedom of the press

The nerve damage, stillbirths and deformities due to thalidomide began to occur in 1957. In this country, fifteen years later the facts were still sealed in a legal cocoon. No public inquiry, no Parliamentary or governmental investigation, no full-scale litigation in the courts, had ventilated causes and responsibility.

The poem of a thalidomide child, Catherine Purkis, conveyed reproach by its quiet pathos:

> Thalidomide makes people stare
> Thalidomide means people care,
> It stops me plaiting my own hair
> It even rules the clothes I wear.
> Thalidomide means Normans Bay
> Where we all go on holiday,
> With children who can also say
> Thalidomide made me this way.
> Thalidomide means Lady Hoare,
> Meetings and parties (which I adore)
> And talks of claims and talk of law
> That must go on for evermore.[1]

Evermore? Leaving everything to the lawyers must have seemed an inadequate solution after ten years. But who could and would intervene? Since the matter was technically before the courts, interference with this process might be in breach of the ancient laws of contempt of court.

Intervention there was, and, in spite of the laws of contempt, it was effective. Members of Parliament, the Government, commercial interests, and shareholders in Distillers all played a part, but pre-eminently it was an achievement of the press. The Phillimore Committee said:

> We have no doubt ... that the change in the course of the thalidomide proceedings which occurred in the months following September 1972 was the result of the campaign of moral pressure against Distillers triggered off by the first two articles in the *Sunday Times*.[2]

It has been suggested, with some plausibility, that the press in this country may not be particularly effective in determining what we think, but they are strikingly successful in determining what we think *about*. In the 1960s both *The Daily Mail* and *The Sunday Times* occasionally featured the plight of the children, keeping the case intermittently in the public eye, but little more. When in December 1971 *The Daily Mail* published an article taking a rather stronger line, it actually prompted complaints from the parents' side that it might jeopardise the negotiations with Distillers.

The *Sunday Times* campaign

The negotiations continued, and continued. The *deus ex machina* was *The Sunday Times*, whose editor decided in 1972 to campaign more forcefully, risking a confrontation with the law. The campaign was to become one of the most famous in the recent history of journalism.

Campaigning journalism is best suited to the Sunday newspapers, who have less opportunity, and less obligation, to report the news of the moment than the dailies. *The Sunday Times* was the foremost of the 'quality' Sundays in terms of reputation and circulation (which in the 1960s had risen to 1½ million, or a readership of about 4 million). It also enjoyed complete editorial freedom under the benevolent proprietorship of Lord Thomson.[3]

The recipient of that freedom was Harold Evans, editor since 1967. At the Darlington *Northern Echo*, Evans had established himself as the country's leading provincial editor and had led a crusade for the posthumous pardon of Timothy Evans. On coming to *The Sunday Times*, Harold Evans envisaged it as leading public opinion on a whole range of libertarian issues: his first two leaders as its editor advocated a new race relations law and a relaxation of the abortion laws. Another facet of the Evans style was involved in the campaign: a willingness to challenge the law, in the interests of freedom of expression to push it to its limits or even, since these are often uncertain, to risk transgressing them. The same boldness had already been shown in 1967 when he disregarded a 'D notice' and courted possible prosecution under the Official Secrets Act by publishing a report on the Philby affair which discussed the British intelligence services. It was later to be demonstrated again over the Crossman diaries.

Harold Evans has said: 'If you're going to stand up to the bully boys of this world, then you need the muscle of a big newspaper'. In the face of the odds, the thalidomide campaign could not be half-hearted or transient. It was neither. Through the autumn and winter of 1972 the pressure was sustained by leaders, articles, and weekly columns appearing under the motif 'Our Thalidomide Children' – a personalised reminder of the nation's responsibility. Articles illustrating the plight of the children and their families appeared in many issues, as well as letters from the parents; Professor Harry Street, a leading tort lawyer, wrote an article entitled 'Why we Must Change the Laws of Compensation'; the progress (or lack of it) in the negotiations with Distillers was reported;[4] in December the editor allowed some pages of one issue to resemble a telephone directory (notoriously unexciting reading material!) by listing some 200 of the major shareholders in Distillers. *The Sunday Times* has spent more that £30,000 on the campaign.

There was, then, a sustained campaign designed to influence the outcome of the thalidomide actions or their settlement out of court. A newspaper's freedom to publish, however, is not absolute but is subject to legal restrictions. In particular, interference with ongoing actions may constitute the crime of contempt of court. The strategy adopted by *The Sunday Times* at the suggestion of their chief legal adviser, James Evans, was to conduct a bipartite campaign. In the first part, arguments would be adduced on moral grounds and without prejudice to legal liability. At a later stage there would be an inquiry into how the tragedy occurred; inevitably this would involve discussion of liability. It was hoped that the first stage would suffice to obtain a satisfactory settlement and that in that stage the laws of contempt would not be infringed.

The issue of 24 September 1972 exemplifies the 'moral argument' approach. The leading article said:

[The] thalidomide children shame Distillers. It is appreciated that Distillers have always denied negligence and that if the cases were pursued, the children might end up with nothing. It is appreciated that Distillers' lawyers have a professional duty to secure the best terms for their clients. But at the end of the day what is to be paid in settlement is the decision of Distillers, and they should offer much, much more to every one of the thalidomide victims. It may be argued that Distillers have a duty to their shareholders and that, having taken account of skilled legal advice, the terms are just. But the law is not always the same as justice. There are times when to insist on the letter of the law is as exposed to criticism as infringement of another's legal rights. The figure in the proposed settlement is to be £3·25 million, spread over 10 years. This does not

67

shine as a beacon against pre-tax profits last year of £64·8 million and company assets worth £421 million. Without in any way surrendering on negligence, Distillers could and should think again.

The same issue contained a three-page article, 'Our Thalidomide Children: A Cause for National Shame', which was sent to all the members of the Houses of Parliament. This article criticised the present mode of assessment of damages, and the system of liability based on fault. It also summarised the position reached so far and criticised again the offer by Distillers of £3·25 million, 'a little more than 1 per cent of the money made in the ten years since thalidomide'.

Distillers complained to the Attorney-General that these articles were in contempt of court, but Harold Evans argued in reply that nothing in them constituted contempt and the Attorney-General decided not to take any action. (Distillers might have brought proceedings for contempt themselves, but did not.)

In a footnote to the article of 24 September, it was stated: 'In a future article the *Sunday Times* will trace how the tragedy occurred'. The draft article in question was submitted to the Attorney-General for his observations on whether publication of it would be in contempt. Distillers, to whom a copy was also sent, suggested it would. The Attorney-General, who may act in the public interest to bring before the court any matter which he thinks may amount to contempt of court,[5] decided to apply to the High Court for an injunction to restrain publication of the proposed article. In effect, there was to be a prior judicial decision on the legality of the article.

This particular article has still not been published, but it was described in these terms by the Lord Chief Justice in the High Court proceedings:[6]

> It suffices, we think, to say that the article is clearly the product of many years of work, and that it traces the history of the development, marketing and testing of thalidomide from the very earliest times and in very considerable detail.
>
> The article does not purport to express any views as to the legal responsibility of Distillers for the sufferings of the children concerned, but it is quite clear that it is in many respects critical of Distillers and charges them with neglect in regard to their own failure to test the product, or their failure to react sufficiently sharply to warning signs obtained from the tests by others. No one reading the article could, we think, fail to gain the impression that the case against Distillers on a footing of negligence was a substantial one.

The article suggested that Distillers brought the drug on to the market without due care (though it also summarised the arguments which might be made on behalf of Distillers), but it did not purport to show that they would be liable – this would depend on it also being established that Distillers owed the unborn children a duty of care. In other words, evidence, or prejudgement, was put forward on one major issue in the pending actions – or affecting the pending settlement of them out of court.

The article was written by Mr Phillip Knightley, an experienced journalist. In his evidence to the Divisional Court in the contempt hearing, Harold Evans promised that, in the event of publication of the article being allowed and their being sued for libel by Distillers, they would plead its truth as a defence. Their confidence stemmed from the fact that 'it was capable of being substantiated on every salient point by documents originally emanating from Distillers themselves'.

The truth of a publication is no defence if it constitutes contempt of court.

Contempt of court and the press

> The Star Chamber and licenser of printing have disappeared, but there still remains over the press of this country one disciplinary jurisdiction almost as stern and far-reaching in its peculiar domain as that of the Star Chamber. It is that of the judges to punish those who print or publish matter declared to be in contempt of court.[7]

The author was neither an outraged journalist nor a revolutionary, but a lawyer writing in 1900 in that most august of legal journals, the *Law Quarterly Review*. The severity of the contempt power has not diminished perceptibly with the passage of time, for the editor of the London *Evening Standard* wrote recently, 'I probably spend more time worrying about the possibility of contempt of court than I do about all the other legal restrictions put together'.[8] The peculiar nature of the crime and the uncertainty as to what constitutes contempt are to blame.

The peculiarity of the crime of contempt lies firstly in its summary nature – it is tried without a jury. This was a power usurped by the judges upon the dissolution of the Star Chamber, which had previously punished contempts; it is now so long-established that its legality is unchallengeable. Not only is the accused denied a jury trial, but he may be tried by the judge who has been the victim or whose court's impartiality or effectiveness has been threatened. A contemnor may be fined any amount and may be imprisoned for any length of time. There was not even any right to appeal against a finding of criminal contempt until the enactment of the Administration of Justice Act 1960. It is also exceptional for a common law crime like contempt (as opposed to statutory offences) to be one of strict liability — that is, it may be committed even though criminal intent is lacking. Generally in criminal law, some 'mental element' such as intent or recklessness or knowledge of the circumstances has to be proved. But an article which could influence a pending action may be in contempt even if the writer neither intended that nor knew anything of the proceedings.[9] Contempt apparently also involves vicarious liability: not only the writer of an article, but the editor or the proprietors are liable to be punished.

Some of these peculiarly harsh features of the crime of contempt of court were absent, of course, in the *Sunday Times* case, where the Attorney-General was seeking not to *commit* an alleged contemnor for his crime but to *prevent* the commission of a crime, if such it would be. His application to the court for an injunction gives the *Sunday Times* case the unusual character of civil proceedings where the issue involved is the commission of a crime.

The principal vice of the law of contempt of court is its uncertainty. That criminal offences should be well-defined in advance is one of the hallmarks of a civilised society. Lord Reid in the *Sunday Times* case agreed that the uncertainties of contempt were a 'reproach' to the law,[10] and Lord Diplock commented that there was 'a dearth of rational explanation or analysis of a general concept of contempt of court which is common to the cases where it has been found to exist'.[11] Primarily this is because there are many forms of contempt and no limit to the ways in which these may be committed. Thus there is an abundance of decisions by lower courts on whether particular actions or publications are in contempt, but judges have preferred not to fetter their successors by creating precedents which *limit* what may be considered in contempt. It has aptly been described as 'the Proteus of the legal world, assuming almost infinite diversity of forms'.[12] Moreover, since the law of contempt is founded on public policy, its ambit must adjust to changing conditions and public opinion. In most areas of the common law, there is a crystallisation of the rules when appellate courts give considered, authoritative judgements. But, as we have seen, appeals in criminal contempt have been possible only since 1960.

In any area of the criminal law it is disturbing when the boundaries are vague. Where criminal penalties operate to limit freedom of expression, the problem is especially serious, for it has rightly been said that there is no more effective censor than an uncertain law. The influential organisation Justice (a politically independent body of lawyers whose aims are to strengthen the rule of law and to improve the administration of justice) published its first report, *Contempt of Court*, in 1959. Its conclusion was that 'the present state of the law tends particularly to impede free discussion in those newspapers and other organs of public opinion which are most responsible, while others tend to treat the law of contempt less seriously'.[13] Nothing had changed materially by 1965 when a joint report by Justice and the British Committee of the International Press Institute, *The Law and the Press*, found a wide divergence of views among newspapermen as to when the law of contempt inhibited comment, but 'almost general agreement . . . that the restrictions imposed by the law of contempt were greater than they appeared because of uncertainty as to their precise extent, especially in view of the need to make quick decisions'.[14]

The law of contempt[15]

The authority and functioning of the legal process is protected by the laws of contempt of court. In the classic definition, contempt is constituted by: 'any conduct that tends to bring the authority and administration of the law into disrespect or disregard, or to interfere with or prejudice parties litigant or their witnesses during the litigation'.[16] Disobedience to an order of the court made in civil proceedings is civil contempt of court. Criminal contempt, the more important category, has four main forms. First, it may be committed 'in the face of the court', as where a judge is physically attacked or the court proceedings disrupted. Secondly, there is conduct or publication which 'scandalises the court' – scurrilous abuse of judges or imputations of partiality. In this century the courts have extended the limits of permissible criticism, on the view that justice should not be a cloistered virtue, but one exposed as hardy enough to withstand attack.[17] Thirdly, it is contempt to victimise a person such as a witness or juror for the part he has taken in legal proceedings, for example by dismissing him from office on account of the evidence he had given. Fourthly, conduct liable to prejudice particular criminal or civil proceedings constitutes contempt. The making public of information or opinion by the news media on a case once it is *sub judice* is the prime example.

When does a case become *sub judice*, so that the possibility of contempt by prejudicing it arises? The first official step in criminal proceedings is the charge or the service of a summons. In a civil action, it is the issue of a writ. But, as a judge once observed: 'It is possible very effectually to poison the fountain of justice before it begins to flow'.[18] The courts, therefore, have taken the view that there may be a contempt when proceedings are 'imminent', even if not yet launched, in a number of cases involving criminal proceedings. (The most famous was wheñ David Frost interrogated Emil Savundra on television a few months before he was charged with fraud.)[19] In principle the position should be the same for civil proceedings, though there is less authority for this point. Civil proceedings are *sub judice* once the writ is issued, at least. It is because of this rule that the problem of 'gagging writs' arises – writs which are aimed at stifling further comment when there is no genuine intention of bringing the action to court.

Publications jeopardising the fair trial of persons accused of crime are regarded as the most serious of all contempts. The interests of society as well as of the individuals concerned are at stake; it is of the utmost importance both that the innocent should go free and that the guilty be convicted. If a line has to be drawn between freedom to publish and the right to a fair criminal trial, the English courts have favoured the right to a fair trial. Thus anything tending to impair the court's impartiality or prejudice its ability to find the true facts is a contempt. In October 1967 *The Sunday Times* described Michael Abdul Malik as having had 'an unedifying career as brothel keeper, procurer and property racketeer,' while he was in fact awaiting retrial on a racial incitement charge. Times Newspapers were fined £5,000 for the offence.[20] A much more notorious case occurred in 1949 when Haigh was in custody on a murder charge, and *The Daily Mirror* ran a front-page story describing him as a 'vampire' and stating that he had committed other murders. Silvester Bolam, the editor, was imprisoned for three months, and the company fined £10,000.[21]

In one contempt case concerning criminal proceedings, the judge observed that because the case involved was a criminal one, it was 'probably more strictly the duty of the court to prevent any interference with the course of justice than in civil cases'.[22] The differences between criminal and civil proceedings add strength to the view that contempt should operate less harshly with regard to the latter: in civil proceedings, the state is not directly involved and the possible consequences for the parties are less drastic – their liberty is not at stake. Whereas the principal aim of the prevention of prejudice to criminal trials is that the jury enters upon its task free from bias, civil trials are usually tried by judges alone.

Only about 2 per cent of civil actions are jury trials, and actions for personal injury must normally be tried by a judge alone.

Harold Evans made the point forcefully in his Granada Guildhall Lecture in 1974:

> In thalidomide we at the *Sunday Times* have been challenging contempt of court in a civil case where no jury trial is likely, where no one's liberty is at stake. It ought to be unthinkable that we cannot analyse or discuss or argue the facts about something that happened nearly thirteen years ago for the simple reason that the courts are said to be seized of the matter. Some seizure.[23]

As Evans implies, there is not in fact appreciably greater freedom to comment on civil proceedings than on criminal, despite the differences between the two. Contempt is equally committed whenever the court's impartiality is impaired, when witnesses are influenced or deterred from giving evidence, or where there is a deliberate attempt to prejudice a case. Additionally, since in civil actions parties have a choice as to whether or not they bring, proceed with, and defend actions, the course of justice is interfered with if when they do so a publication seeks to influence them unfairly.

It is clear that as regards publications about civil proceedings too, the protection of justice, and not freedom of expression, remains the master value. A judge in one of the cases said:

> The right of the press to comment on any matter of general public interest, as long as the comment is fair comment, is a matter of very great public interest, but it is a right which is subject to certain restrictions, one of which is that the organs of the press must not be used in any way to prejudice the proper trial of actions in the courts of the country, that being a higher public interest.[24]

The *Sunday Times* case

The general description above of the law of contempt should not be taken as invalidating the previous criticisms of its uncertainty. The bland statement that a publication which *prejudices* the proper trial of an action is in contempt is not in itself very helpful. What one still needs to know is *when a publication does so prejudice.*

This is where the uncertainty lies, and where it is prejudice to civil proceedings that is in issue, there are relatively few reported cases, presumably because criminal proceedings catch the attention of the news media with more frequency. In the *Sunday Times* case, therefore, the courts had the unenviable task of deciding what the law was in an area where the precedents afforded only limited help, while in the full glare of publicity from the media, which by now were interested not only in the thalidomide case but also in the extent of the restrictions on their freedom to publish.

The Attorney-General's application for an injunction to stop *The Sunday Times* publishing their article on the making and testing of thalidomide was made to the Queen's Bench Division of the High Court, where it was heard in November 1972 by the Lord Chief Justice (Lord Widgery), Mr Justice Melford Stevenson and Mr Justice Brabin.

The court's collective judgement was given by Lord Widgery.[25] It was to the effect that the injunction should be granted, and *The Sunday Times* restrained from publication. The court thought there were three principal ways in which the requirement of fair trial might be prejudiced: first, by prejudicing the mind of the tribunal itself though professional judges were much less likely to be affected in this way than were jurymen; secondly, by deterring or influencing witnesses; thirdly, by affecting the free choice or conduct of a party to proceedings. The present case was not concerned with the first kind of prejudice, nor with the second, since any scientific witnesses would scarcely be influenced by a newspaper article.

But there were some precedents, which the court relied on, indicating that it was contempt to put pressure on a party to an action. An eighteenth century Lord Chancellor had said:

> There may also be a contempt of this court, in prejudicing mankind against persons before the cause is heard. There cannot be anything of greater consequence, than to keep the streams of justice clear and pure, that parties may proceed with safety both to themselves and their characters.[26]

Given that prejudicing a party might be contempt, what was the test of whether it *was* contempt? The court said it was 'whether the words complained of create a serious risk that the course of justice may be interfered with'. In their judgement, the proposed article did involve such a risk.

It has been observed that contempt may be committed even where there is no intention to interfere with the course of justice. In fact such criminal intent or *mens rea* is not a necessary, but is virtually a sufficient, condition.[27] Acts or publications intended to interfere with imminent or pending proceedings constitute contempt, even where there is no risk of actual or potential prejudice. The second ground of the court's decision against *The Sunday Times* was this: that the newspaper was seeking to mobilise public opinion on the children's behalf in order to affect the outcome of the proceedings or settlement. The evidence which Harold Evans gave in an affidavit made this clear: 'I therefore came to the conclusion that it was in the public interest that I should publish the draft article and that if I delayed doing so until after the final settlement of all claims against Distillers the article would not be of any benefit to the children'.

On both of those grounds, the draft article would be in contempt if published, the court said. The main argument put forward in defence had been that even if there was prejudice to the administration of justice, there was also a public interest in being informed of matters of importance, and that the courts should weigh these competing public interests in the balance before deciding if there was a contempt. This suggestion, that the right to know might outweigh the prejudice to proceedings, had never been accepted by an English court, though an Australian case supported it.[28] The Divisional Court flatly rejected it.

The same Divisional Court, immediately after the hearing of the *Sunday Times* case, went on to hear an application from the Attorney-General to commit London Weekend Television Ltd. for contempt of court in respect of a programme they had televised about the thalidomide case.[29] These were criminal proceedings.

On Sunday 8 October 1972 the television company devoted a programme in the *Weekend World* series to the plight of the thalidomide children. Their chief executive (Mr John Freeman) was aware of the contempt of court danger; in consequence, following the example of *The Sunday Times*, he directed that the programme should be aimed only at establishing a moral case, and should avoid comment on legal liability. Changes were made accordingly in the compilation of the programme, one of which was the deletion of an interview with a Swedish lawyer describing the settlements obtained by the children there. Instead, a commentary was broadcast which attempted to précis part of the interview, but in doing so it misrepresented the nature and amount of the Swedish payments, to which the Distillers offer was unfavourably compared. There was also a rather one-sided presentation of the views of some Distillers' shareholders.

The Attorney-General argued that the intention behind the programme was to shame Distillers publicly with a view to influencing the proceedings, and that the programme was likely to do so. The court applied the same rules of law as in the *Sunday Times* case, but with a different result. Here the judges found that the intention of those responsible had been to avoid committing contempt, and any prejudice caused would have been careless, not deliberate. And while the programme created a risk of interference with the course of justice, it was not a *serious* risk, because it was shown only once and those parts which might be objected to had not in the court's view made very much impact.

The view of the law taken by the Divisional Court in these two cases was entirely predictable. It followed the guidelines laid down in earlier decisions. In fact, by the system of precedent which operates in this country, the Divisional Court is bound to follow its previous decisions, or those of higher appellate courts. The Court of Appeal and the House of Lords, however, are very much freer, and the *Sunday Times* case went on appeal to those two courts. Their freedom arises from their power to disregard or overrule precedents from lower courts (and in the case of the House of Lords, their own too). Because of the lack of reported appeals in cases of contempt – the House of Lords indeed had *never* previously considered the subject in modern times – this freedom was almost absolute, on any view of the legal system. The Realist approach to jurisprudence, which has been fashionable in this century, would stress that in most cases judges exercise value preferences; the apparently binding legal rules prove to be chimerical, only one variable to be adopted, rejected or bent at will. This is an extreme view of the judicial process, but one which often appears plausible, as in the present case. Indeed Lord Justice Scarman in the Court of Appeal frankly admitted that they were dealing with an area where 'discretion is a major element in the process of decision'.[30] Given this position, it is interesting to contrast the Court of Appeal's approach in this case with that of the House of Lords. John Griffith, Professor of Public Law in the University of London, has argued persuasively that the temper and philosophy of the two courts are seldom in accord, and that the present House of Lords is predominantly 'conservative', stressing the private rights of the individual, while the Court of Appeal is more 'activist', being more concerned with social justice.[31]

The Court of Appeal and the House of Lords on contempt

The Sunday Times appealed against the judgement of the Divisional Court to the Court of Appeal. The appeal was heard by Lord Denning, Lord Justice Phillimore (the chairman, at the time, of the committee appointed to consider whether changes were required in the law of contempt), and

Lord Justice Scarman. In February 1973 the Court of Appeal unanimously allowed the appeal and removed the injunction.[32] They held that (1) the test of prejudice to proceedings was whether there was a real and substantial danger of prejudicing pending litigation being actively pursued, and here the litigation was dormant rather than active; and (2) in addition to the private interest of the parties in a fair trial, there is a public interest in matters of national concern and the freedom of the press to make fair comment on them. These interests must be balanced against each other, and if the public interest in the freedom of speech is the stronger, as in the circumstances here, there is no contempt.

The court was also much influenced by the fact that Parliament, which purportedly adopts the same *sub judice* rule as applies elsewhere, had on 29 November 1972 debated the plight of the thalidomide children and touched on some of the issues dealt with in the banned article. Because of the legal privileges enjoyed by Parliament, anything said in the course of business there may also be reported freely in the press with immunity from proceedings for libel or contempt. Following that debate in the House of Commons, there was a spate of newspaper editorials, articles and letters on the case, [33] including a *Daily Mail* article on 8 December which Lord Denning described as being on much the same lines as the one banned. In the light of these developments, the Court of Appeal thought it would be unrealistic to maintain the injunction.

The Attorney-General appealed against the decision of the Court of Appeal, and in May 1973 the case was heard by the House of Lords (Lord Reid, Lord Morris, Lord Diplock, Lord Simon and Lord Cross). This court unanimously reversed the decision of the Court of Appeal and reimposed a ban.[34]

The judges in the House of Lords did not attach much importance to the debate in Parliament. Lord Cross pointed out that it had concentrated almost entirely on the moral obligations of Distillers, which put it on the same plane as the article *The Sunday Times* had published on 24 September.[35]

As for the unpublished article, the Lords of Appeal found publication would be a contempt because (1) publications prejudging specific issues in a case which is before a court for determination are in contempt; and (2) for this purpose, negotiations for a settlement were to be viewed in just the same way as a trial, and the case could not be regarded as dormant. Lord Morris and Lord Simon also noted that the deliberate aim of affecting proceedings would render the article contemptuous.

A summary of the reasoning of the judges in these two courts cannot entirely do justice to the complexities of eight separate judgments. (The academic lawyer's task is much simpler in those foreign countries where appellate courts deliver their reasons in a single judgement!) Furthermore, the judges in the House of Lords took the opportunity to consider and restate the law of contempt more widely than was necessary to dispose of the case before them.

The views of the higher courts on contempt may be considered more fully under four headings: active and dormant proceedings; the test of contempt; influencing a party to proceedings; the public interest.

Active and dormant proceedings

Here there is an undoubted liberalisation of the law. It was previously thought that the *sub judice* rule would prevent or punish prejudicial comment from the time that proceedings were imminent until they had been finally concluded. But the Court of Appeal was most emphatic that the law of contempt did not inhibit comment when litigation is dormant and not being actively pursued. The courts differed over how the thalidomide case was to be classified for the purpose of this test. The Court of Appeal took the view that 'so far as the courts are concerned, these actions have gone soundly to sleep and have been asleep for these last three or four years'.[36] The House of Lords said that although nothing had been done in court, 'active negotiations for a settlement were going on all the time'.[37] What the House of Lords did not challenge was the existence of the rule.

The overwhelming majority of civil actions are disposed of by settlement out of court, not by litigation, and the law of contempt affords equal protection to the two processes. Given the present law, the interpretation of the facts by the House of Lords appears to have been the more realistic. Negotiations were not dormant. They had certainly been slow until November 1972, when the Divisional Court delivered its judgement, but between then and the Court of Appeal's judgement, Distillers increased their offer on two occasions, and a third offer which formed the basis of the settlement agreed was made before the House of Lords decided. Perhaps it was the Court of Appeal's object to restrict the contempt protection to actual litigation. If so, this would have represented a radical departure from the law as previously understood, and the House of Lords had none of it.

A compromise solution would be to provide that comment could only be contemptuous if published after a case had actually been 'set down' for trial. Such a reform was widely advocated by the press following the decision of the House of Lords. Newspapers were aghast that the judges were neither shocked nor dismayed by the slowness of proceedings; a statement by Lord Cross that 'in this case . . . the parties are trying in the early stages of the litigation to reach a settlement'[38] rankled with the editorial staff of *The Times*.[39]

The test of contempt

It had been thought that publications which created a serious risk of prejudice to the fairness of a trial were in contempt. The Court of Appeal formulated the test as 'a real and substantial danger of prejudice' to the trial or settlement of the case.

The House of Lords did not deny that publications involving such dangers were in contempt, but laid down that publications which prejudged a case or specific issues in it were in contempt, whether or not any risk of prejudice was involved. Such prejudgements were regarded as intrinsically objectionable: the function of the courts would be usurped, the parties would lack protection, disrespect for the process of the law would follow. An absolute rule was necessary in order to prevent a slide towards trial by newspaper or television.

The rule that any public prejudgement of an issue being litigated is contemptuous, even where there is no chance that the fairness of the trial would be affected, came as an unpleasant surprise to the media. In extending so far, the rule seems unnecessarily harsh. Investigative journalism, which has had its outstanding successes, is seriously impeded. If newspapers enquire into the causes of an airline disaster, the collapse of a building or an international fraud, is the possibility that court proceedings may follow to deprive them of their right to publish? Is there not sometimes a *duty* to publish?

Influencing a party to proceedings

The ruling on dormancy and prejudgement would have sufficed to dispose of the case in the House of Lords. But the court was invited by the Attorney-General to compare with the banned article *The Sunday Times* of 24 September with its articles seeking publicly to pressurise Distillers by stating the moral arguments against them. Their Lordships took the opportunity to clarify when it would be illegal to put pressure on a litigant.

Here too, if narrowly, there was a bonus for free speech. Previously it was thought that pressure on a party to proceedings was contemptuous if it carried a serious risk that his conduct in the proceedings would be affected, or that was intended. This, it will be recalled, was the basis of the decision in the Divisional Court, on the ground that it was prejudicial to the course of justice. However, Lord Reid observed that 'the fact that a party refrains from seeking to enforce his full legal rights in no way prejudices a fair trial whether the decision is or is not influenced by some third party. There must be absolute prohibition of interference with a fair trial but beyond that there must be a balancing of relevant considerations.'[40]

There was agreement that exposing a litigant to public abuse or execration was unlawful. But Lord Reid and Lord Cross declared that fair and temperate criticism designed to influence a litigant was permissible, provided that there was no prejudgement of the issues or endangering of the fairness of the trial (and there was neither in the article of 24 September). Lord Morris, too, agreed with this; Lord Diplock and Lord Simon specified only what was unlawful, and this might be interpreted as implied agreement. By a majority at least, responsible comment directed at a party is allowed.[41]

Between fair and temperate criticism and public execration there are no doubt many gradations, and their Lordships differed as to when the line dividing lawful from unlawful comments should be drawn. Most would seem to allow any *private* persuasion provided it is not otherwise illegal (i.e. bribery), but Lord Simon would not accept even private pressure on a litigant as permissible save within narrow limits.

There was also disagreement over classifying the article of the 24 September issue. Lords Reid, Cross and Morris found it unobjectionable. Lord Diplock and Lord Simon, far from regarding it as fair and temperate, decided, 'it does hold Distillers up to public obloquy for their conduct'.[42] This divergence will occasion publishers and editors some difficulty in their attempts to derive practical guidance from the case.

The public interest

The public's 'right to know', served by the freedom of the press, weighed heavily with the Court of Appeal. The judges there were clear that there must be a balancing of this interest with the interest in preventing interference with the administration of justice, and that sometimes freedom of speech would take priority. The thalidomide case presented a unique combination of features: a national tragedy, no public inquiry, no litigation likely, untoward delay in settlement. In such circumstances the public interest in discussion should prevail.[43]

The Court of Appeal's approach was warmly welcomed by the media, though the emphasis on the *uniqueness* of the thalidomide case might have limited its value as a precedent.

In the House of Lords only lip-service was paid to the balancing approach. 'I agree with the Master of the Rolls [Lord Denning] that the law must hold these two interests in balance', said Lord Simon; but later: 'To attempt to strike anew in each case the balance between the two public interests . . . would not be satisfactory'.[44] Instead, a simple line is drawn, and 'free' speech starts where the laws of contempt of court (and defamation, obscenity, official secrets and so on) stop. 'There can be no such thing as a justifiable contempt of court', said Lord Morris.[45] This is the traditional ambit of the protection of liberties in this country; freedoms are not guaranteed but residual: they exist only in so far as they are not taken away. This is not balancing, for one is already weighed and found wanting.

In a recent leading textbook on the law of contempt, Miller argues strongly that the House of Lords was wrong to reject the public benefit defence:

> Admittedly such a defence would introduce an element of uncertainty into the law. Yet it is also the case that certainty must surely be acquired at too high a price if prejudicial comment published during the restricted *sub judice* period is necessarily to be designated a contempt.
>
> A number of examples might be taken. The most obvious is perhaps the case envisaged in the 1959 *Justice* Committee report of a newspaper which seeks to protect the public by publishing a photograph of a dangerous criminal who is on the run. The *Justice* committee thought that it would be 'nothing short of folly' to regard such a publication as a contempt, and few would disagree . . . . Again, it might also be argued that the protection of the financial well-being of sections of the public might occasionally be sufficiently important to negative liability for contempt. Indeed it is cases of this nature which create most of the problems in practice for those who work in the field of investigative and financial journalism. For example, the Business News section of the *Sunday Times* frequently publishes stories setting out the past criminal record of persons currently promoting new business enterprises . . . Beyond this it might be argued that discussion of matters of genuine international concern, such as Watergate or the massacre at My Lai, cannot sensibly be required to be suspended once a libel action has been set down for trial. The same must surely have been true of the thalidomide case had Distillers continued to market the product and had the *Sunday Times* published an article pointing to the causal connection between the drug and phocomelia.[46]

One might agree that these kinds of publications should not be prosecuted as contempts without supporting a public benefit defence. One way to deal with such problems, used to some extent at present, lies in the discretion afforded to prosecuting authorities. A more satisfactory technique which might virtually dipose of the need for such a defence would be to place a limit on *when* something may be in contempt and *what*, in that period, will be contemptuous. This was the approach taken by the Phillimore Committee.

The Phillimore Report[47]

From time to time, as it becomes evident that some area of law or administration should be reformed, the government of the day appoints a committee to make recommendations. Commonly the subsequent report is accepted as the basis of legislative or policy changes, sometimes it is put aside to gather dust.

In June 1971, the Lord Chancellor appointed a committee on contempt of court. The uncertainty in this area of the law was particularly pronounced, and its procedural features were anomalous; the advent of newspapers with large circulations and the development of radio and television had made the potential harm to the administration of justice that much greater. If the setting up of a committee was long overdue, not a great deal of public interest was evinced at the time. Within a few months, however, contempt was in the headlines as a result of cases before the controversial and short-lived National Industrial Relations Court, and *The Sunday Times* was beginning its thalidomide campaign.

With this backcloth, the Phillimore Committee went about its business of gathering and considering evidence. The Committee was ill-starred; one member, Lord Grant, died in 1972, to be replaced by another Scottish judge, Lord Cameron, and Lord Cameron acted as chairman during the later stages when Lord Justice Phillimore became seriously ill. After the House of Lords had decided against *The Sunday Times* several members of Parliament pressed for the report to be speeded up, but circumstances delayed publication until December 1974.

The report deals with the whole law of contempt of court, in Scotland as well as in England. The premises which influenced the committee's recommendations are made explicit. A law of contempt is required because there is a continuing need to protect the administration of justice. Since however the summary procedure for punishing contempt deprives the accused person of many of the safeguards normally enjoyed by other offenders, it should be invoked as little as possible — only where the offending act does not fall within the definition of any other offence, or where necessity requires the matter to be dealt with in this way. In pursuit of these aims, the committee proposed a 'hiving-off' of some areas from the existing law of contempt: victimising a witness or juror after he has taken part in legal proceedings should be made a new separate offence; contempt by scandalising the court should be abolished and replaced by a new offence of defaming a judge in such a way as to bring the administration of justice into disrepute; contempt in the face of the court should be referred to prosecuting authorities to be dealt with as another criminal offence (e.g. assault) where possible.

Clarification of the law of contempt was thought desirable, as well as restriction. The committee found that it fell short of the certainty it ought to have, especially in those areas affecting the press. The *Sunday Times* case had not helped greatly:

> There is no better illustration of the present uncertain state of the law than the variety of judicial opinion expressed in the *Sunday Times* case itself. That case was considered by three courts: the Divisional Court of the Queen's Bench Division, the Court of Appeal and finally the House of Lords. The judgements and reasoning in each court disclose a remarkably wide variety of routes by which the judges reached their decisions. There is nothing very unusual in the reversal by a higher court of a lower court's decision, but such a variety of judicial reasoning is exceptional, especially in a matter where penal sanctions are involved.[48]

The thalidomide case was referred to extensively by the committee, for they devoted their attention chiefly to the area of conduct or publications prejudicing particular proceedings.

Where there is conduct (or publication) *deliberately* in order to prejudice particular proceedings, such as bribing a juror or threatening a witness, this amounts to contempt and also another criminal offence, that of perverting or obstructing the course of justice. The committee recommends that this should remain so, but that the conduct should be dealt with as a contempt only if it occurs after proceedings have started and before they are completed. Of course *The Sunday Times* deliberately tried to affect the outcome of the thalidomide actions by putting pressure on Distillers, as in the leading article of 24 September 1972. In the view of the Divisional Court the aim rendered the article contemptuous. In the view of the House of Lords, the legality of pressure on a party depended on whether it was to be characterised as fair and temperate criticism or public abuse. Here the committee proposes a change. Parties to proceedings, unlike judges, jurors and witenesses, are not fulfilling a public duty. It is recommended therefore that conduct directed against a litigant in connection with legal proceedings in which he is concerned should not be criminal unless it amounts to intimidation or unlawful threats. In the view of the committee neither this form of contempt nor the offence of perverting the course of justice should be constituted unless there is an intention *wrongfully* to interfere, and moral suasion of a party should fall outside this test. Indeed the committee went so far as to say:

> What lent the *Sunday Times* campaign so much strength was the fact that in the eyes of many people justice and the administration of the law in the thalidomide case were two very different things. We think there is great force in the argument that this is a legitimate matter for public comment.[49]

Next the committee turned its attention to publications unintentionally creating a risk of prejudice. This is the area which worries editors most: the report of an accident or a crime may state details subsequently at issue in legal proceedings; investigative journalism by its nature uncovers malpractices and abuses which frequently become the subjects of prosecutions or actions; matters of public discussion like battered babies or the obscentity laws may also be the ingredients of particular proceedings at the time. This is the area of strict liability; if the publication is sufficiently prejudicial to be contemptuous, it matters not whether there was any intention of interfering with a trial or action.

The proposals made by the committee, if enacted, would significantly restrict the ambit of this strict liability. First, it is suggested that the strict liability form of contempt should only apply to publications (defined as 'any speech, writing, broadcast or other communication, in whatever form, which is addressed to the public at large') and not to conduct of any other kind. Anything else done would not amount to contempt unless it is deliberate interference.

With regard to publications, the committee sympathised with the complaints of the media:

> It may be that the right to issue . . . publications must on occasion be overridden by the public interest in the administration of justice, but we consider that the balance has moved too far against the freedom of the press. Moreover, it cannot be right that publications should be stifled simply because the law of contempt is uncertain.[50]

Two principal reforms are suggested to redress the balance and introduce greater certainty, a redefinition of the test of contempt and a limitation of the time during which the press is at risk.

It is proposed that a standard definition of contempt should be provided by statute. Prejudgement of issues in pending proceedings, to which the House of Lords took objection, is not considered by the committee to constitute an adequate test. Actually a careful reading of the Lords' judgements suggests that they did not put that forward as a comprehensive test to replace the 'serious risk of prejudice' formula, but intended it to be an addition. At all events the Phillimore Committee prefers a single test based on a modification of the traditional formula. The test should be 'whether the publication complained of creates a risk that the course of justice will be seriously impeded or prejudiced'. This test shifts the emphasis from the degree of risk to the degree of harm. Since only the danger of *serious* adverse effects would be relevant, the field of liability would be considerably narrowed.

Further, the committee recommends that the concept of the imminence of proceedings (as the time when the law of contempt begins to bite) should be buried. Where the proceedings are criminal, strict liability should date from the charge or the service of a summons; where the proceedings are civil, it should commence only when the case has been set down for trial. The enactment of this proposal would entail that 'shadow boxing dressed up as litigation' would not enjoy the protection of the contempt laws. It would also reduce the proportions of the 'gagging writs' problem, where writs are issued for the sole purpose of stifling comment when there is no genuine intention to bring an action. One member of the committee, the television personality Mr Robin Day, would have gone further. In a note of dissent, he suggests that for civil proceedings comment should be permissible until shortly before the trial.[51] A *sub judice* list could be available, on which cases would appear one or two weeks before the hearing, and contempt liability would date only from the time of appearance on the list. The committee unanimously recommends that the law of contempt should cease to apply at the conclusion of the trial or hearing at first instance, both in criminal and civil proceedings, except where a rehearing or new trial is ordered.

Since these proposals together would effect a marked restriction of liability for contempt, it is perhaps not surprising that the committee decided not to recommend the creation of a general defence of public benefit. There is much force in the view that because public benefit is notoriously difficult to define, its inclusion in the law of contempt would militate against the professed aim of making the law more certain. Courts are charged with the task of weighing public interests in a few areas such as obscenity, breach of confidence, and requiring production of evidence from the Crown, but decisions have inevitably had mixed receptions. However, the committee did recommend that it should be a defence to show 'that a publication formed part of a legitimate discussion of matters of general public interest and that it only incidentally and unintentionally created a risk of serious prejudice to particular proceedings'.

The Sunday Times described the Phillimore recommendations as 'restrained',[52] but the report was generally welcomed by the media, and, it is submitted, rightly so. Major relaxations of the law would result from legislation in accordance with the proposals.

The *Sunday Times* case in 1973, under such a law, would have had a different result. Since proceedings had not started, there could be no deliberate contempt. Since no action had been set down for hearing; strict liability would not apply and the possibility of prejudice would be irrelevant. (Even if an action had been set down, if it was to be tried by a judge without a jury, would there be a risk of serious prejudice? The committee's view on this point is not at all clear.)

The articles published by *The Sunday Times* discussing the laws of compensation and fault liability would clearly come within the 'legitimate public discussion' defence even if published after an action was set down.

The articles which criticised Distillers for failing to fulfil their moral responsibility would be entirely outside the scope of contempt if any pressure on a litigant short of illegal actions were permissible.

The Phillimore Committee suggested that such of its proposals as were acceptable to Parliament should be referred to the Law Commission for statement in legislative form. So far Parliament has not acted.

Contempt and human rights in Europe

Legislative changes along the lines of the Phillimore Committee's recommendations may be hastened by another development: Harold Evans submitted a complaint to the European Commission of Human Rights at Strasbourg that the House of Lords decision to ban the proposed article on the mertis of the thalidomide case was in breach of the European Convention for the Protection of Human Rights and Fundamental Freedoms.[53]

This Convention is the offspring of the Council of Europe, born in the heady post-war atmosphere of European *entente* when the evils of unbridled nationalism were fresh in the memory and the menace of a new totalitarianism loomed in Eastern Europe. The Universal Declaration of Human Rights adopted and proclaimed by the United Nations in 1948 was to remain an unenforced statement of principle, but the like-minded democracies which formed the Council of Europe enshrined their ideals in a new and enforceable charter. The Convention was signed in 1950 and came into force in 1953. It guarantees human rights such as the right to life, freedom from torture and freedom from slavery; it guarantees traditional civil liberties such as freedom of religion, freedom of assembly, and freedom of expression. Most of the guarantees are not absolute; when individuals are grouped in a democratic social order, the exercise of rights implies also a duty not to infringe the rights of others and a sense of responsibility to society. Many of the Articles therefore require a delicate judgement as to how far restrictions of freedom are legitimate in a democracy, and Article 10, which Harold Evans alleges has been violated, is of that kind:

> 1 Everyone has the right to freedom of expression. This right shall include freedom to hold opinions and to receive and impart information and ideas without interference by public authority and regardless of frontiers. This Article shall not prevent States from requiring the licensing of broadcasting, television or cinema enterprises.
> 2 The exercise of these freedoms, since it carries with it duties and responsibilities, may be subject to such formalities, conditions, restrictions or penalties as are prescribed by law and are necessary in a democratic society, in the interests of national security, territorial integrity or public safety, for the prevention of disorder or crime, for the protection of health or morals, *for the protection of the reputation or rights of others*, for preventing the disclosure of information received in confidence, or *for maintaining the authority and impartiality of the judiciary.*

The eighteen Council of Europe states which have ratified the Convention are obliged to secure to everyone within their jurisdiction the rights and freedoms specified. In many of the countries, the guarantees in the Convention were made directly part of the national law upon ratification, and in some others they have been incorporated into national law by legislation. In the United Kingdom this has not happened. But the practical effect should be the same: we are bound by our ratification to ensure as a minimum that our national law is in conformity with the Convention. Changes in our law have been required or encouraged as a result, in such fields as immigration, the Prison Rules, and appeals procedure. If, therefore, there is eventually found to have been a violation of the Convention through the House of Lords decision and the wrong is held not to have been redressed, there will be a judgement against our government, which would then be obliged to amend the law. There is no ultimate sanction by which this international law can be enforced, certainly, but only compliance is compatible with continuing membership. The pressures are those of international reputation and public opinion.

Evans brought his complaint against the British Government in January 1974 and in March 1975 the Commission ruled that it was admissible.[54] Though this was merely a preliminary decision which does not prejudge whether there has been any violation of the Convention, it is an important first hurdle, for 95 per cent of complaints are dismissed at this stage as being groundless or outside the Commission's jurisdiction or competence. Evans welcomed the decision, saying he hoped the Government would be forced to implement the Phillimore recommendations, 'and bring some sense to the ridiculous laws of contempt'.[55]

His delight was premature, for a lengthy process remains, with the eventual result uncertain. The Commission's role is now investigative and conciliatory, as defined by Article 28:

> (a) it shall, with a view to ascertaining the facts, undertake together with the representatives of the parties an examination of the petition and, if need be, an investigation, for the effective conduct of which the States concerned shall furnish all necessary facilities, after an exchange of views with the Commission;
> (b) it shall place itself at the disposal of the parties concerned with a view to securing a friendly settlement of the matter on the basis of respect for Human Rights as defined in this Convention.

Often a payment by the state concerned to the individual complainant has constituted the 'friendly settlement' and the Commission has regarded that as satisfactory. But the *Sunday Times* complaint was clearly not amenable to settlement in this way.

On 11 and 12 December 1975 the Commission heard evidence on the case both from the *Sunday Times* representatives and from those of the British Government. Its task of negotiating a solution continues, but after the evidence is heard a report on the facts is drawn up in which the Commission gives its view as to whether the state is in violation of its obligations and, if it is, proposes how these obligations might be met. The report has the character of an opinion, and not a judgement, and is not made in public. But if the opinion is that there was violation and if the violation has not been made good, the matter may be referred to the European Court of Human Rights – made up of as many judges as there are member states of the Council of Europe – either by the Commission or the state concerned. If not referred to the Court, the matter goes instead to the Council of Ministers (the executive organ of the Council of

Europe, made up of the foreign ministers of each of the states, or their deputies). In either case, there follows an official judgement as to whether or not there has been a violation, which is made public.

Clearly, it is a long drawn out process. A final decision by the Court may well be made five years after the original complaint. How the *Sunday Times* case will be decided is difficult to predict. The crucial point is whether the ban on the article was *necessary for the protection of the reputation or rights of others or for maintaining the authority and impartiality of the judiciary*. Unfortunately there have been very few decisions on alleged violations of Article 10, and none at all on the meaning of those particular phrases. The case might fairly be described as involving a very moot point. If anything, this tilts the balance slightly in favour of the British Government; other things being equal, states with democratically-elected legislatures are presumed to act in good faith, and the Commission will not readily offend national sensitivities. The jurisprudence of the Commission establishes that there is a 'margin of appreciation' allowed to state authorities.

The complaint to the European Commission will serve its purpose, of course, if it helps to spur the Government to legislative action.

Confidence and copyright: the ban reinforced

When Distillers complained to the Attorney-General's office about the *Sunday Times* articles of 24 September 1972, the newspaper was asked for its observations. Harold Evans attempted to justify the articles already published as being within the law. He also sent a copy of the article not yet published which was to become the subject of the contempt proceedings. He said of it:

> I should be very grateful for any observations you may have upon it. You may take it that we are entirely satisfied with its factual accuracy in every respect but it is our intention to give representatives of the parties to the litigation the opportunity of commenting thereon before making a decision as to whether to publish it.[56]

On 10 October the draft article was handed to the chairman of Distillers. Only then did Distillers become aware that the newspaper was in possession of documents or copies of documents which belonged to them. By a writ of 2 November 1972 Distillers sought to recover them, claiming that quoting from their documents would be contrary to the copyright laws and that even indirect reporting of their contents would constitute breach of confidence. *The Sunday Times* undertook in reply that for the time being they would make no use of the documents other than for the purpose of taking legal advice in the proceedings. Distillers were content with this, since by then the Attorney-General had in any case decided to test whether the article would be in contempt of court. There were a number of attacks on the article.

Following the judgement on the House of Lords on contempt, the newpaper's lawyers began preparing arguments on the law of copyright and the law of confidence, and on 4 March 1974 they wrote to Distillers' lawyers to revoke the undertaking. Distillers applied to the court for an interim injunction to restrain the use or disclosure of the documents by the newspaper, and the application was heard in chambers by Mr Justice Talbot in June. (Only part of the judgement was allowed to be published.)[57]

Throughout the contempt proceedings, Times Newspapers maintained that the article told the simple truth. The points made in the article were, after all, substantiated by details taken from Distillers' own documents. But, as has been said, truth is never pure and rarely simple. A witness in court has to swear to tell the whole truth, for what is true may not be the whole truth. Mr Justice Talbot said:

> Perhaps the principal reason why the plaintiffs complain of the defendants' use of their material is that the defendants are unfairly critical, that they have misreported the documents which they have used, that they have selected information from the documents to support their criticism of the plaintiffs and that they have suppressed other material which has relevance to the matters contained in the defendants' critical article . . . It seems to me that, on the evidence, all these matters have been proved.[58]

The newspaper's handling of evidence does not seem to have been beyond reproach. Nor was the way in which the documents were obtained.

How did *The Sunday Times* come into possession of Distillers' documents? In late 1967 Harold Evans met Dr Montague Phillips. Phillips was a chemist who had been retained by Kimber, Bull as a technical adviser on the thalidomide litigation. His own wife had contracted peripheral neuritis as a result of taking thalidomide, and he seems to have felt strongly that proper care by Distillers would have prevented the tragedy. On 6 February 1968 Dr Phillips entered into an agreement with *The Sunday Times* whereby he would supply them with all the information (documentary or otherwise) which he possessed on the case in return for £5,000. Evans intended to use the information in the production of newspaper articles and later a book. Dr Phillips had some 10,000 of Distillers' documents relevant to the making and marketing of thalidomide; these were photocopied by the newspaper and the originals then returned to Phillips.

But the documents had only reached Phillips because of the pre-trial process of discovery. In a civil suit, once the parties have served the pleadings on each other, lists of documents are exchanged. These lists enumerate all the documents in the possession of each party which might be relevant to the case. The documents are produced for inspection by the opposing party, who may copy them. If necessary, disclosure may be compelled by the court. Distillers had disclosed on discovery about 30,000 documents in the action *S* v. *Distillers*,[59] of which the solicitors for the parents who were claiming bespoke about 10,000. Naturally the solicitors handed these over to their adviser Dr Phillips. When Distillers discovered this late in 1968, their solicitors wrote to Phillips asking for an undertaking that he would not use the documents for publication of any kind. Phillips replied, giving such an undertaking. He concealed the fact that he had already sold copies of them to a newspaper. Shortly afterwards, Phillips died. It was clear to Harold Evans that the documents had been obtained only as a result of the process of discovery. There might, however, be a higher public interest at stake than the protection of legal processes. This was what Times Newspapers tried to argue.

The court was primarily concerned with the question of confidence. The action for breach of confidence is a civil remedy affording protection against the unauthorised disclosure or use of information which is of a confidential nature and which has been entrusted to a person in circumstances which impose an obligation to respect its confidentiality.[60] An award of damages may punish a breach, or an injunction may prevent one. The broad principle is clear, and was applied in a number of nineteenth century cases. Most cases have involved commercial or industrial information, but in recent years the courts have been asked to prevent disclosure of other kinds of information. In one case, for example, the Duchess of Argyll obtained an injunction restraining her former husband and *The People* newspaper from revealing in public marital confidences she had entrusted to the Duke during their marriage.[61]

The courts will only protect information which has the necessary quality of confidence about it and only where there exists an obligation of confidence regarding it. However, even when these conditions are present, there may sometimes be a higher public benefit in disclosure than in the preservation of the confidence. The Court of Appeal has recognised this explicitly by affirming in several cases that there is a defence of public interest, which if successful would legalise the breach.[62] Lord Denning M.R. has explained its scope – where disclosure is justified – as follows:

> It extends to any misconduct of such a nature that it ought in the public interest to be disclosed to others ... The exception should extend to crimes, frauds and misdeeds, both those actually committed as well as those in contemplation, provided always – and this is essential – that the disclosure is justified in the public interest.[63]

Public interest is obviously a very flexible concept. In another case, Lord Denning said the judge who had to decide whether to grant an injunction should 'look at the whole case ... and then decide what is best to be done'.[64]

Mr Justice Talbot decided it was best to restrain publication. He accepted the submissions on behalf of Distillers that there was an implied legal obligation imposed on a party not to make improper use of discovery documents, and that confidentiality was all the more necessary because the documents were compellable by court order. Anyone who received such documents could be in no better position than the recipient of the confidence if he knew their origin to be the product of discovery. There were clear authorities in support of these propositions.

A lack of protection for discovery documents might endanger the proper functioning of the process, so one aspect of the public interest was the need to protect the due administration of justice. Judges might be expected, indeed, to make this consideration paramount. We have seen that it weighed heavily with the House of Lords in the contempt proceedings, and Mr Justice Talbot was likewise impressed by it. Could any higher public advantage be gained by allowing disclosure? Certainly the matter in the documents, the judge thought, was something 'in which the public is deeply interested'. But he held that the conduct of Distillers was outside the categories of exceptions; *even if* negligence could be proved, this would not be a sufficiently grave misdeed to justify the publication of confidential information. And the judge's view of the passages in the newspaper's draft article was that they were 'innacurate'.[65] In all the circumstances he found that the higher public interest was served by protecting the plaintiffs' right to confidentiality.

Another plank of Distillers' argument was based on the law of copyright. Clearly copyright in the documents was theirs. But *The Sunday Times* would have a defence to this objection if either their purpose was fair dealing for the purposes of criticism or review, under section 6(2) of the Copyright Act 1956, or if it was fair dealing for the purpose of reporting current events in a newspaper, under section 6(3). The judge decided that there could be no fair dealing by criticism unless documents had been published or at least widely circulated, and that the events described in the documents were no longer current events.

The injunction will remain in force until a court orders otherwise. *The Sunday Times* did not appeal on this occasion. The hearing before Mr Justice Talbot was only for an *interim* injunction. At the time of writing, *The Sunday Times* has not returned the documents, and there may still be a trial of the action to recover them, when the issues would be fought out again.

The lifting of the contempt ban

On 23 June 1976, the Attorney-General applied to the Divisional Court to discharge the contempt injunction which he had successfully sought in 1972–73. Having been announced only a few days previously, the move came as a surprise.

It was explained in court that the public interest no longer demanded the Attorney-General's intervention. Almost all of the thalidomide claims against Distillers had been settled. Only four actions were extant, and those only technically: in one where the pleadings stage had been completed in 1974 no steps had been taken since; the other three had never reached that stage. The hearing of the Attorney-General's application had lasted only four minutes when Lord Widgery, the Lord Chief Justice, indicated that the court had heard enough. Because the 'pending' proceedings were in fact dormant, the injunction was discharged.

The Attorney-General may have acted solely for the reasons explained in court. But another possible motivation is the threat of an adverse decision in Strasbourg. Was the Report by the European Commission of Human Rights critical of the contempt ban? If so, the lifting of the ban may be sufficient to sway the Commission or the European Court of Human Rights the other way, or it may even be regarded as a 'friendly settlement' of the matter, since on one view no grievance now remains.

Distillers might themselves have tried to persuade a court that the possibility of prejudicing proceedings still existed, but the Divisional Court's expedition in discharging the Attorney-General's injunction would hardly have encouraged them, and they did not. However, the injunction restraining *The Sunday Times* from using Distillers' documents was unaffected. Harold Evans wrote to Sir Alexander McDonald, the chairman of the Distillers Company, after the Divisional Court hearing requesting a release from this court order, but Sir Alexander replied:

> I note that the Attorney-General's injunction against Times Newspapers Limited has been discharged by the Divisional Court. You are aware of the terms of the injunction granted by Mr Justice Talbot on July 31, 1974, in connection with our confidential documents bought by your company from Dr Phillips. I must ask you to ensure that this injunction is strictly observed.

The newspaper was therefore free to publish the thalidomide story subject to the laws of libel and of confidence in respect of Distillers' documents. It was, said the newspaper, 'the first full account of a tragedy that need never have happened'. The story appeared at the first opportunity, in the issue of 27 June, under the title, 'Thalidomide: The Story They Suppressed'; the article covered six full pages, and amounted to almost 20,000 words. It described the discovery and marketing of thalidomide by Chemie Grünenthal, the state of scientific knowledge and drug testing generally in the late 1950s, the warning of Dr McBride in Australia, and the response to the tragedy by the Ministry of Health and legal institutions. What had to be *omitted* as a result of the breach of confidence injunction, according to Mr Phillip Knightley, interviewed on television that evening, were details of how Distillers had come to the decision to market the drug here, what testing they did on animals and what clinical trials were held.

The thalidomide case and press freedom

The *full* thalidomide story, therefore, may never be told. If courts ascribe the quality of legally enforceable confidentiality to many situations, this would constitute a much more serious limitation on freedom of expression than has been realised, though there are some who would favour such limitations in the interest of privacy. Legislation to circumscribe definitively the ambit of the law of confidence is desirable, and may be expected since the Law Commission has turned its attention to this area. There is unlikely to be any change in the general principle of protection for discovery documents, nor would many support such a change.

The history of thalidomide raises wider question about the freedom of press comment. Reform of the law of contempt may have been hastened, but meanwhile the present law has a wide reach. Are the restrictions it imposes necessary, or even effective? If not, the freedom of speech ought to prevail.

One lesson to be drawn from the thalidomide case history is that the law of contempt is not always effective in preventing outside influence and comment. Mr Robin Day has noted:

> If the campaign against Distillers was a serious interference with the course of justice, the law of contempt was unable to prevent it. The campaign was waged in the press, on television, and in Parliament. The House of Commons had relaxed its own *sub judice* convention. This meant that newspaper and broadcast reports of Parliament included comment which might otherwise have led to contempt proceedings. There was pressure from important institutional share-holders. The boycotting of Distillers' products was threatened. Despite the suppression of the *Sunday Times* article, the campaign of protest and pressure made a mockery of the law of contempt.[66]

Parliament's intervention, being privileged from the law of contempt, could not be unlawful. From the judgements in the House of Lords on the question of seeking to influence a litigant, most of the other pressures mentioned by Day would also seem to be lawful, although that was not so clear at the time. Some of the press comment on the other hand, not all of which was adverse to Distillers, was of doubtful legality when viewed against the 'prejudgement' test. Two examples favourable to the company's case may be cited. A *Daily Telegraph* article of 8 January 1973 said: 'It should also be emphasised that though Distillers are morally responsible they were not in any normal sense of the term negligent. At the time it was standard medical dogma that the foetus was effectively isolated'. On the same day, the *Daily Express* publicised a statement by a director of Distillers: '. . . we were not negligent . . . We went though all the necessary tests at the time. We could not have done more'.

Whether within the law or not, a great deal was written about the case, and there were attempts from different quarters to influence the litigants. But only one, unpublished, article was prohibited as a result of proceedings, and by the time these were concluded the volume of pressure, most of it directed against Distillers, had generated sufficient force to transform the outcome of the case, regardless of the law of contempt.

If there are some occasions when the law of contempt is ineffective, there are others where its severity could be injurious. Harold Evans, in his

Granada Guildhall Lecture in 1974, provided an instructive illustration:

> There is a scandal in the land. There is no sight of the substance of it, only the smell of something rotten. A newspaper makes inquiries. Painstakingly it builds up a dossier. It is about to publish a series of articles which give a glimpse of some of the truth when the law intervenes. The newspaper's facts, it is said, have some bearing on a series of legal cases which are technically before the courts. No trials have yet begun but until they have and until they are concluded, which in all their aspects may be several years, nothing can be published . . . It would be punishable as contempt of court; it would be a grievous abuse of the freedom of the press.
>
> I am referring to Watergate: and I am describing what would have happened if Washington had been London. The first whiff of the scandal in the land was on the night of 17 June 1972, when five men with bugging equipment were caught in the offices of the Democratic national committee. From that moment, had Washington been London, the rules of contempt of court, the cry of *sub judice*, would have deterred independent press inquiry and prevented publication of any results. In Washington, however, the *Washington Post* was free, under American law, to play a major part in uncovering the scandal and it seized it brilliantly.[67]

A sceptic might argue that a Watergate here would be dealt with by questions in Parliament. But such a response would only be possible if the members of Parliament *knew* some of the relevant information. In fact Parliament, like the rest of use, relies on the press for much of its knowledge. This was stressed by the then leader of the Opposition, Mr Harold Wilson, writing to *The Times*, after the House of Lords judgement on contempt, on 23 July 1973:

> Parliament is hamstrung in its discussions of, and decisions on, matters of public importance if it cannot draw both on the facts and opinions freely published in the press . . . For the raw material of parliamentary debate is in fact what members read in the press . . ..
>
> Therefore, if the law is as the Lords have authoritatively stated, Parliament . . . has not only the right but the duty to change it.[68]

The greater freedom enjoyed by the press in the United States[69] arises from the provision in the Constitution that Congress 'shall make no law . . . abridging the freedom of speech or of the press'. The freedom is not absolute, but courts have been denied the power to hold publications in contempt unless there has been a 'clear and present danger' to the administration of justice, and in practice this formula has been very restrictively interpreted. The American view has been that a fair trial depends on the efficient administration of justice, not on muzzling the press. Some protection is afforded through the jury selection process, the postponement of trials or change of venue, and sequestration of juries. These techniques may be more expensive and less efficient than a strong law of contempt and British commentators have generally disparaged them. But greater use of such methods is worth considering if an unbiased jury can be obtained without censoring the press.[70] We might also place more faith in the ability of jurors to dismiss extrinsic factors from their minds, for there have been striking examples in recent years of cases in which a jury has acquitted in spite of its knowledge of previous convictions, notably in the Kray and Janie Jones trials. In so far as the neutrality of juries is the justification of the law of contempt, it should be remembered that presently in this country about 98 per cent of both criminal and civil actions are tried without juries.

There are dangers to the administration of the law if the law of contempt is so radically altered as to free the press entirely. But in a case like thalidomide the administration of the law and *justice* may be perceived as two different things. There are dangers to an open and just society if we restrict the right to know.

Notes

[1] *The Sunday Times* 18 November 1973.

[2] Report of the Committee on Contempt of Court, HMSO 1974, Cmnd. 5794, para.60.

[3] Harold Evans has said of Lord Thomson that he has never commented on a single editorial policy: see H. Hobson, P. Knightley and L. Russell, *The Pearl of Days*, Hamish Hamilton 1972, p.472. The book is an anecdotal history of the *Sunday Times* newspaper.

[4] Some of these, as well as the judgements in the contempt proceedings, are reprinted in the report published by the newspaper, *The Thalidomide Children and the Law*, André Deutsch 1973.

[5] The Attorney-General's discretion to intervene when the proceedings are civil was doubted by the Court of Appeal in *Attorney-General* v. *Times Newspapers Ltd.* [1973] 1 Q.B.710, but confirmed by the House of Lords: *Attorney-General* v. *Times Newspapers Ltd.* [1974] A.C.273.

[6] *Attorney-General* v. *Times Newspapers Ltd.* [1972] 3 All E.R.1136,1140.

[7] A.E. Hughes, 'Contempt of Court and the Press', *Law Quarterly Review*, vol.16, 1900, p.292.

[8] C. Wintour, *Pressures on the Press*, André Deutsch 1972, p.129.

[9] *R. v. Odhams Press Ltd., Ex parte A.-G* [1957] 1 Q.B.73. But the strict liability is now mitigated in some respects by s.11 of the Administration of Justice Act 1960.

[10] [1974] A.C.273, 294.

[11] Ibid., 308.

[12] J. Moskovitz, 'Contempt of Injunctions, Civil and Criminal', *Columbia Law Review*, vol.43, 1943, p.780.

[13] Justice, *Contempt of Court*, Stevens 1959, p.39.

[14] Justice, *The Law and the Press*, Stevens 1965, para.20.

[15] See generally G.J. Borrie and N.V. Lowe, *The Law of Contempt*, Butterworths 1973 (a comprehensive survey of the law), and C.J. Miller, *Contempt of Court*, Elek 1976 (a more recent and critical account).

[16] J.F. Oswald, *Contempt of Court*, Butterworths (3rd ed.), 1910, p.6.

[17] See Miller, *Contempt of Court*, ch.10. In other countries at least, this part of the contempt laws may still be used repressively: see L.A. Powe, 'The *Georgia Straight* and Freedom of Expression in Canada', *Canadian Bar Review*, vol.48, 1970, p.410.

[18] Wills, J. in *R. v. Parke* [1903] 2 K.B.432, 437.

[19] *R. v. Savundranayagan and Walker* [1968] 3 All E.R.439.

[20] *R. v. Thomson Newspapers Ltd., Ex Parte A.-G* [1968] 1 All E.R.268.

[21] *R. v. Bolam, Ex parte Haigh* (1949) 93 Sol.Jo.220.

[22] Cozens Hardy, J. in *Re New Gold Coast Exploration Company* [1901] 1 Ch.860, 863.

[23] Granada Guildhall Lectures 1974, *The Freedom of the Press*, Hart-Davis, MacGibbon 1974, p.26.

[24] Buckley, J. in *Vine Products Ltd. v. Green* [1966] Ch.484, 495.

[25] [1972] 3 All E.R.1136.

[26] Lord Hardwicke, L.C., in *The St. James Evening Post Case* (1742) 2 Atk.469, 471.

[27] *R. v. Duffy, Ex parte Nash* [1960] 2 Q.B.188.

[28] *Ex parte Dawson* [1961] S.R.N.S.W.573.

[29] [1972] 3 All E.R.1146.

[30] [1973] 1 Q.B.710, 747.

[31] J.A.G. Griffith, 'Judges, Race and the Law', *New Statesman* 22 November 1974.

[32] [1973] 1 Q.B.710.

[33] See *The Thalidomide Children and the Law*, pp.76–8.

[34] [1974] A.C.273.

[35] Ibid., p.324.

[36] [1973] 1 Q.B.710, 738, *per* Lord Denning, M.R.

[37] Ibid., p.301, *per* Lord Reid.

[38] Ibid., p.323.

[39] *The Times* 19 July 1973.

[40] [1974] A.C.273, 296.

[41] Ibid., *per* Lord Reid at pp.297–8, Lord Cross at p.326, and Lord Morris at p.307.

[42] Ibid., p.313 *per* Lord Diplock.

[43] The Court of Appeal has again treated public interest as a defence in *Wallersteiner* v. *Moir* [1974] 3 All E.R.217. See J.H. Farrar and N.V. Lowe, 'Fraud, Representative Actions and the Gagging Writ', *Modern Law Review*, vol.38, 1975, p.455.

[44] [1974] A.C.273, 319.

[45] Ibid., p.302.

[46] Miller, *Contempt of Court*, pp.153–4.

[47] *Report of the Committee on Contempt of Court*, HMSO 1974, Cmnd. 5794. There is a summary of recommendations, pp.92–6. See also D.G.T. Williams, 'Contempt of Court: Possible Reforms', *Cambridge Law Journal*, 1975, p.6.

[48] *Phillimore Report*, para.7.

[49] Ibid., para.61.

[50] Ibid., para.102.

[51] Ibid., pp.98–100.

[52] *The Sunday Times* 4 August 1974.

[53] See generally F.G. Jacobs, *The European Convention on Human Rights*, Oxford 1975, and F.E. Dowrick, 'Juristic Activity in the Council of Europe – 25th Year', *International and Comparative Law Quarterly*, vol.23, 1974, p.610.

[54] Decision of the Commission as to the Admissibility of Application No.6538/74.

[55] *The Times* 8 April 1975.

[56] *The Thalidomide Children and the Law*, p.39.

[57] *Distillers (Biochemicals) Ltd.* v. *Times Newspapers Ltd.* [1975] 1 All E.R.41.

[58] Ibid., at p.45.

[59] [1969] 3 All E.R.1412.

[60] See generally The Law Commission, *Breach of Confidence*, Working Paper No.58, HMSO 1974, which contains a useful summary of the present law.

[61] *Duchess of Argyll* v. *Duke of Argyll* [1967] Ch.302.

[62] *Fraser* v. *Evans* [1969] 1 Q.B.349, *Hubbard* v. *Vosper* [1972] 2 Q.B.84.

[63] *Initial Services Ltd.* v. *Putterill* [1968] 1 Q.B.396, 405.

[64] *Hubbard* v. *Vosper* [1972] 2 Q.B.84, 96.

[65] *Distillers (Biochemicals) Ltd.* v. *Times Newspapers Ltd.* [1975] 1 All E.R.41,50.

[66] *Phillimore Report*, pp.99–100.

[67] *The Freedom of the Press*, pp.21–2.

[68] See also H. Street, 'Could English Law Cope?', *New Law Journal*, vol.124, 1974, p.796.

[69] See R.L. Goldfarb, *The Contempt Power*, Columbia University Press 1963. However at the time of writing the contempt laws are before the Supreme Court for review in the *Simants* case.

[70] See R.L. Goldfarb, 'Public Information, Criminal Trials and the Cause Célèbre', *New York University Law Review*, vol.36, 1961, p.810.

4 The pharmaceutical industry and its control

The freedom of the press to explore the causes of a tragedy may be vital in a democracy, but it is usually the avoidance of such tragedies in the future that is the public's chief concern. Could there in fact be another drug disaster comparable to thalidomide? Has the industry put its house in order? In this chapter we shall attempt to answer these questions. In the final chapter we consider whether the legal system would now cope any better with such a tragedy, and, if not, how it might be enabled to.

The pharmaceutical industry

In 1961 the population of the United Kingdom relied entirely on the pharmaceutical industry for the safety of medicines. To some extent we still do.

This industry became organised only at the beginning of the century. Pasteur's advances in bacteriology and immunology, and the German scientist Ehrlich's discovery of *Salvarsan*, a drug to treat syphilis, in 1907, laid the foundations for the coming age of chemotherapy. Improved techniques of industrial manufacture facilitated quality control and mass production, and many firms engaged in related fields began to make prescription medicines. Professor L.J. Henderson of Harvard selected 1912 as the first year in human history 'in which the random patient with a random disease consulting a random physician had a better than 50—50 chance of benefiting by the encounter'.[1] But it was in the 1930s that the drug revolution really got under way. In 1932 Bayer's chief pharmacologist, Domagk, cured his daughter's septicaemia with the dye *Prontosil.* Within months, the active ingredient was found to be sulphanilamide, and the drug companies were off on the search for allied compounds, with riches in prospect. It was May and Bakers's sulpha-drug, *M & B 693*, which saved Churchill's life when he contracted pneumonia in North Africa in 1943. 'The intruders', he said, 'were repulsed'. Meanwhile penicillin, discovered by Fleming in 1928, had been manufactured in bulk by American companies, and in the post-war years new and more effective antibiotics such as the tetracyclines were developed. In the 1950s oral diuretics became available to treat heart disease, steroids for skin disease, asthma and arthritis, and drugs to reduce high blood pressure. In recent years hormones have provided oral contraceptives, and psychotropic drugs have been developed and used widely to treat the effects of mental illness and depression. In the last fifteen years there have been signs that the stream of important new drug discoveries is drying up and significant breakthroughs may now be expected to arrive less frequently. The nature and complexity of the serious physical diseases of present times, such as heart disease (responsible for more than a third of deaths in this country) and cancer (responsible for one death in five) are such that no 'wonder drug' could be expected to wipe them out. With the limits of the drug revolution coming into view, it is time to take stock and put its achievements, its failures, and its price, into perspective.

Whether the expenditure of billions of pounds and the vast input of human and physical resources by the drug industry have resulted in great improvements in public health is a vexed question. The measurement of illness in the community is complicated by social factors. Thus days off work for certified illness per 100 men in Great Britain increased from 1,279 for 1954 to 1,632 in 1967, that is by 27 per cent.[2] Apparently our health is deteriorating. In fact these figures may reveal more about changing attitudes to work and to tolerance of illness. Even 'hard figures' showing a reduction in deaths from particular diseases are often hard to interpret, for many diseases seem to wax or wane unpredictably over a period of time. In 1935 there were 3,690 deaths in this country from diphtheria and scarlet fever; in 1970 there was one death from scarlet fever and none from diphtheria.[3] The introduction of antibiotics which could defeat these diseases in the 1940s was no doubt *one* factor. But in 1935 the death rates for these diseases had already fallen to less than one-sixth of those in 1860, so that a graph for the period 1860–1970 shows the decline in deaths as a practically straight line, hardly altered by the introduction of antibiotics. By far the most impressive achievement in public health is reduced infant mortality. In 1900 one child in seven died in the first year of life, today the figure is less than one in fifty. A child born in 1870 had an average life expectancy of 40 years, a century later the average expectancy was about 70 years.[4] Undoubtedly improved medical care, including the new pharmaceutical products, has contributed to this, but so have improved sanitation, better control of the purity of foods, increased prosperity, better nutrition, smaller families and other environmental factors. Life expectancy when calculated at age 45 has improved only very slightly (by about 6 years) since 1870, despite the pharmaceutical revolution, and in some Western countries has now begun to decrease slightly. Dr John Powles, of the Centre for Social Research at the University of Sussex, has written:

> One of the more striking paradoxes facing the student of modern medical culture lies in the contrast between the enthusiasm associated with current development, and the reality of decreasing returns to health from rapidly increasing efforts.[5]

Some of the claims made by pharmaceutical industry are clearly of the *post hoc, propter hoc* kind, and should be regarded with caution. On the other hand, there is clear evidence of positive gain in some areas. Thus the treatment of tuberculosis by drugs has been very successful: in 1925 the disease caused more than 40,000 deaths in this country, now this has been reduced to less than 2,000 per year. And with microbic infections generally, there is a close correlation between the development of appropriate antibiotics and much higher cure rates. Credit must also be awarded for the extent to which many who are ill are enabled to 'feel better'. For example, modern medicines have transformed the daily lives of many who suffer from diabetes, asthma, rheumatism, and various psychiatric disorders.

There is much on the credit side, yet the pharmaceutical industry is more virulently attacked than almost any other, so that studies of it are frequently extreme either in praise or denigration.[6] The industry has figured prominently in the demonology of the Labour party since Harold Wilson, as Chairman of the Public Accounts Committee in 1961, denounced its excessive profits and the volume of spending on promotion. But criticisms cannot all be conveniently dismissed (though one writer tries)[7] as emanating from 'advocates of fringe medicine techniques' or 'the political Left – those opposed to the profit motive in principle'. Dr Halfdan Mahler, the Director-General of the World Health Organisation, has recently criticised[8] the bombardment of the medical profession with masses of drugs, advertised at great cost, when 95 per cent of health problems could be solved with a range of less than 200 drugs. 'Part of our bitterness' he attributed to the fact that the drug companies had not yet applied their resources to seeking drugs for certain major diseases, 'because they will not be the big money makers'. Dr Mahler has also criticised the drug companies' practices in the Third World:

> Drugs not authorised for sale in the country of origin – or withdrawn from the market for reasons of safety or lack of efficacy – are sometimes exported and marketed in developing countries; other drugs are promoted and advertised in those countries

for indications that are not approved by the regulatory agencies of the countries of origin. Products not meeting the quality requirements of the exporting country, including products beyond their expiry date, may be exported to developing countries that are not in a position to carry out quality control measures. While these practices may conform to legal requirements, they are unethical and detrimental to health.[9]

Criticisms of the industry in this country have largely been on grounds of high profits or its promotional ehtics. The charge of 'excessive profits' is inevitably an emotive one in the area of health, where in some sense people are 'making money out of the sick'. The issue is particularly sensitive when there is a National Health Service which is the industry's biggest customer, since the drugs bill is borne by all of us. The bill has mounted. In 1958 the cost of prescription drugs to the NHS was £45 million. By 1970, these medicines cost us £170 million, and provisional 1975 figures show the cost as £340 million. This is quite apart from profitable sales of patent medicines to the public over and above these figures.

Drug prices appear astronomically high when compared with basic manufacturing costs. This can be illustrated by comparing prices here with those in 'free market' countries such as Italy and Finland which have no patents on drugs[10]: in early 1973 a kilogram of *Valium* costing £27 in Italy sold in the United Kingdom for £1,260. (Ironically the company derived the name from the word 'value'.) Of course, the manufacturing cost can hardly be taken as a realistic index of a fair price, and the difficulty of finding a fair price formula leaves plenty of room for argument. The firms justify the difference by pointing to their reputation for quality and its cost, the costs of safety and compliance with international regulations, money spent on keeping doctors informed of new drugs, and, especially, research costs. Research is high-risk in that much is spent on work which leads to no marketable product, and, when new medicines are introduced, the volatility of the market makes for product obsolescence. About £40 million was spent on research and development by pharmaceutical companies in this country in 1975, and companies have generally spent between 7 and 13 per cent of total sales on it, with many of the larger ones at the higher level. (But spending on advertising and promotion was £48 million in 1975, or 14 per cent of total sales.) Since 1957 the prices of prescription medicines have been subject to negotiations under a series of Voluntary Price Regulation Schemes operated between the Department of Health and the industry, and two studies in 1964 and 1970 both showed the United Kingdom to be one of the lowest-priced European drug markets.[11]

Voluntary controls, however, do not seem to be enough. Over the last twenty years British governments have intermittently engaged in uneasy confrontations with the pharmaceutical industry. In 1956/57 when there was a 16 per cent rise in the cost of medicines to the NHS, a Committee on the Cost of Prescribing was set up under the chairmanship of Sir Henry Hinchliffe. The Committee blamed doctors for over-prescribing and prescribing expensively, and manufacturers for over-exuberant advertising. In 1961 the Minister of Health (Mr Enoch Powell) surprised the drug companies by invoking section 46 of the Patents Act 1949 (allowing the Government to use patented goods 'for the services of the Crown') to buy for the hospital service cheaper foreign equivalents of some tetracyclines and other widely used drugs. Pfizer challenged the legality of this action unsuccessfully in the courts.[12] In 1965 the Government set up under the chairmanship of Lord Sainsbury a Committee of Enquiry to examine the relationship of the pharmaceutical industry with the National Health Service.[13] It found 'a general picture of reasonableness, but with exceptions, some of them important and serious'. It suggested the abolition of brand names and a reduction in patent protection so that real price competition might be fostered. It thought sales promotion methods were wasteful and sometimes irresponsible. It found that about a third of the prescription drugs on the market were ineffective, and recommended that there should be a licensing system for new drugs. Some of the proposals on safety and advertising were enacted in the Medicines Act 1968.

Ambivalence has characterised the attitude of successive governments to the drug firms. If the state abuses its strength and prices are forced too low, profits may be reduced to the point where research and drug innovation are inhibited. And nothing would be gained by crippling an industry which is conspicuously more successful than others in trade balance terms. In 1975 the export surplus over imports rose steeply to £276 million.[14] The Government's most important attempt to curb prices so far was in fact directed at a foreign company, the Swiss-based Hoffmann-La Roche. After a prolonged series of encounters in the courts, a settlement was reached when Roche agreed to repay £3·75 million excess profit on their non-barbiturate sedatives *Librium* and *Valium*.

In April 1976 a Labour Party policy statement on the industry called for the state (by way of the National Enterprise Board) to take over at least one United Kingdom-owned company with a substantial interest in pharmaceuticals, 'to serve a number of diverse public policy purposes'. At the same time, the Minister of State for Health, Dr David Owen, was negotiating with the industry to secure their agreement to cut promotional spending down to 10 per cent of total sales.

It is clear that the British Government's efforts to control the prices and practices of the pharmaceutical industry has not been determined or sustained enough to be successful. No other country has been very successful either, because of the formidable practical difficulties of intervention. The power of the large pharmaceutical companies derives from their multinational character and their near-monopoly trading position. Sixty-five per cent of the NHS medicine market is controlled by foreign-based companies. The drug industry has more of the *élite* known as multinational firms than any other industry. There is a 'big league' of about fifty multinational giants (including the United Kingdom-based Glaxo, Wellcome, Beecham, ICI and Fisons) which control more than a third of the total world market, a market which, it is estimated, will be worth more than $50,000 million by 1980.[15]

These giants are likely to retain, and probably increase, their exceedingly high degree of market power. Risks are lessened for them because their business is diversified. They have accumulated the available technical, scientific and human resources, and the increasing costs of research and development inhibit the entry of new rivals. Patents systems ensure a minimum of competition for several years and legal or illegal agreements between the major companies can ensure that the minnows are left nothing to bite. Profits are maximised by adjusting operations to take account of different national finance laws, as in the practice known as 'transfer pricing' between subsidiaries.

So far as the economic structure of the industry has any bearing on the degree of legal liability to which it could or should be made subject, it is clear that the pharmaceutical industry is one of high profitability. Its average return on capital employed in this country in 1970 was 18 per cent, compared with 12·5 per cent for manufacturing industry generally. Similarly, in the United States the average return was 18 per cent, compared with 11 per cent for other manufacturing industries, in the period 1960–73. The National Economic Development Office report, *Focus on Pharmaceuticals*, also observed that: 'Profit margins are generally higher for the larger firms because most of them market research-based innovations, which have higher margins than standard products'.[16]

In Western countries there is clear evidence that smaller firms involved in pharmaceuticals are disappearing and not being replaced.[17] Size has become a precondition of survival. It is not unreasonable to anticipate an increasingly profitable market being spread between a decreasing number of firms. In the United States the major drug companies have adjusted relatively painlessly to stricter bases of legal liability. It is a burden which this industry could clearly carry.

Has the high profit motive been paralleled by sufficient concern for the safety of pharmaceuticals? Commercial considerations alone would indicate the necessity of some care. By and large most pharmaceutical companies seem not to have been so irresponsible as to sell products to the public which they knew or suspected to be unsafe. A notorious exception was *MER/29* (triparanol), an anti-cholesterol drug marketed in America between 1960 and 1962 by Richardson-Merrell, the company which hoped to sell thalidomide there. It was later shown that severe side effects revealed by the laboratory research were falsified or concealed in the licence application successfully made to the Food and Drug Administration, and only belated and inadequate warnings were given even as additional data of serious toxicity in humans flowed in. When the company finally took the drug off the market, more than 5,000 of its users had suffered serious side effects such as cataracts, hair loss, impotence and skin reactions. Criminal indictments, and many civil actions, followed.[18]

Apart from the *MER/29* case, drug manufacturers have generally complied with such safety or licensing requirements as exist. But have these requirements been sufficient, and are they now? To attempt to answer this, we must first consider what the risks are.

Drug safety

In a Message on Consumer Protection in 1962, the late President Kennedy summarised the pros and cons of the pharmaceutical revolution:

> The successful development of more than 9,000 new drugs in the last 25 years has saved countless lives and relieved millions of victims of acute and chronic illnesses. However, the new drugs are being placed on the market with no requirement that there will be either advance proof that they will be effective ... or the prompt reporting of adverse reactions. These new drugs present greater hazards as well as greater potential benefits than ever before – for they are widely used, they are often very potent and they are promoted by aggressive sales campaigns that may tend to overstate their merits and fail to indicate the risks involved in their use.

What the thalidomide tragedy did was to awaken the public to, and remind doctors of, the hazards of drug treatment.

Major disasters of the thalidomide kind have been rare. In 1937 a chemist in the United States used a solvent in producing a liquid form of sulphanilamide which turned out to be highly toxic. One hundred and seven people died, plus the chemist, who committed suicide by swallowing his fatal preparation. Improper production of the BCG vaccine caused the deaths of seventy-two children at Lübeck in 1928, and faulty manufacture and testing of the Salk vaccine resulted in 204 cases of poliomyelitis, with eleven deaths, in the United States in 1955.

But these dramatic disasters are merely the prominent tip of the iceberg, being responsible for only a tiny fraction of the illnesses and deaths which pharmaceutical products have caused over the years. Any biologically active substance is capable of doing harm as well as good. As Sir Derrick Dunlop put it: 'Most drugs . . . are given for their pharmacological properties to modify or repress biological processes. Unless they can do this they will be ineffective in treatment, but if they have this attribute they are bound to cause adverse effects from time to time'.[19]

In his book *Drugs, Science and Society*, Dr Alan Norton classifies the risks under four broad headings.[20] First, there are the ordinary side effects, unwanted consequences inherent in the pharmacological actions of the drug. Antihistamines which relieve hay fever also induce drowsiness. Antibiotics prescribed for throat infections may also kill useful bacteria in the intestines, so that diarrhoea develops. Two antibiotics, chloramphenicol and streptomycin, were widely used for relatively trivial infections until practical experience showed that the first could cause a fatal blood disease and the second cause permanent deafness. Even older and long-trusted remedies like digitalis, aspirin and phenacetin are not free from risk: use of phenacetin over a long term can cause kidney damage, while aspirin is a frequent cause of intestinal haemorrhages. A second problem is overdosage, whether through intention or error. Since a near-harmful dose of a drug is often needed before it is effective, the dangers are obvious. There are now good grounds for believing that about 3,500 asthmatics died in England and Wales between 1961 and 1967 from the over-enthusiastic use of pressurised aerosols.[21] After warnings from the Committee on Safety of Drugs in 1967, deaths from asthma fell dramatically. Thirdly, there are risks involved in idiosyncrasy. People vary enormously in their tolerance of drug dosage, both initially and in the longer term. Alcohol provides a familiar example of this. Fourthly, allergic or hypersensitive reactions may be developed. These differ from idiosyncrasy in that the effects are not related to the dose of the drug or to its ordinary pharmacological action. More than 5 per cent of people are allergic to penicillin, so that the drug formerly considered so safe causes several hundred deaths in the world every year. Norton's four classes cover only ordinary therapeutic use. There are also, of course, the problems of industrial poisoning, accidents and suicides. And the volume of drug-taking in technologically advanced societies is such as to exacerbate the problems. Many drugs, of course, produce dependence, rendering them all the more profitable for the manufacturers. When drugs are taken in combination there may be harmful interactions, since the metabolism of one drug may affect another. Sometimes these synergistic effects, such as occur with barbiturates and alcohol or certain antidepressants and cheese, prove fatal. There is now recognition of the commonness of iatrogenic diseases[22] (those caused by doctors and their activities, and sometimes called DOMP, or diseases of medical practice). P.F. D'Arcy, Professor of Pharmacy at the Queen's University, Belfast, told the Royal Society of Health congress in 1976 that a number of studies in Britain showed that between 10 and 26 per cent of patients suffered from diseases induced by doctors.

Enough has been said to show the possible dimensions of the safety problem. The actual figures of drug-induced death and injury must remain a matter of conjecture. Doctors, not surprisingly, are reluctant to ascribe a patient's illness or death to therapy; thus only six deaths of asthmatics were reported as likely to be due to the use of aerosol bronchodilators during 1965 and 1966, a period when, it has now been reliably estimated, they led to 1,700 deaths.

Every act of therapy involves a calculated risk. There can be no absolute standard of drug safety. Essentially the risks of using a drug have to be measured against the harm of not using it, and the standard to be applied should obviously vary with the seriousness of the illness and the condition of the patient. The administration of chloramphenicol to a patient with typhoid, or a drug with known risks to a cancer sufferer, may be justified, when administration as a prophylactic or to deal with a trivial ailment would not. The administration of a drug with *unknown* risks may be less justifiable when the patient is pregnant. These assessments are left to the judgement of the prescriber.

The supporters of the pharmaceutical industry point out that there is an imbalance in society's attitude. Public concern over the safety of medicines is not paralleled by concern over mortality due to surgery; the media often seem obsessed with possible side effects of contraceptive pills to the neglect of the risks in pregnancy; there is official complacency over the dangers of cigarette smoking. There is some validity in these arguments, but they would be easier to accept if we could be confident that drug prescribers invariably do calculate the risks. Professor D.R. Laurence, in his textbook on *Clinical Pharmacology*,[23] suggests that before treating any patient with a drug the doctor should satisfy himself of the following five points:

1   whether he should interfere with the patient at all and, if so,
2   what alterations in the patient's condition he hopes to achieve;
3   that the drug he intends to use is capable of bringing this about;
4   what other effects the drug may have and whether these may be harmful;
5   whether the likelihood of benefit, and its importance, outweigh the likelihood of damage, and its importance.

Does this happen? In this country it is estimated that more than 70 per cent of consultations with general practitioners end with the signing of a prescription, that more than half the adult population and about a third of the child population take some kind of medication every day, and that the leading tranquilliser *Valium* alone is taken by 14 per cent of the population.[24] As Laurence observes, 'habitual polypharmacy is sure to blur the outline of rational thought which should precede the use of any drug'. For this situation the pharmaceutical industry, which has so successfully exploited man's tendency to feel insecure, the medical profession, which has co-operated, and the public, who have succumbed, must share the blame.

Time is a crucial factor in drug safety. With any new drug there is always the element of risk *undiscoverable* at the time. Partly this is a matter of scientific knowledge, partly it depends on practical experience. If a fatal idiosyncratic reaction or allergic effect occurs in only one patient in 10,000, then it is unlikely to be discovered in clinical trials, and there may not be conclusive evidence of the effect for many years. Thus adverse effects may not be recognised as attributable to a drug for a number of years, though they may have occurred. Phenacetin was introduced in 1887, but it was more than sixty years before its effects on the kidney were suspected and it was only in 1975 that over-the-counter sales were stopped in this country. It was four years after the introduction of the mono-amine oxidase drugs for depression that the dangers of eating cheese for patients who were being treated with them were reported. Should the delay in recognition of side effects cause us to delay the introduction of new drugs, or perhaps put them on trial at hospital centres by specialists for several years before making them available for general prescription? The principal argument against this is that delay inevitably means that patients who might benefit from new drugs are denied them. The pharmaceutical companies are eager to market their products as quickly as possible to recoup costs; patent life lasts sixteen years, but often five years may elapse between patenting and marketing while trials are conducted, safety requirements satisfied, and production problems solved. Since the thalidomide tragedy there is some evidence that doctors have been slower to prescribe new medicines, which accordingly take longer to reach their sales peak, while in the meantime competitors may be evolving drugs which are similar but just sufficiently dissimilar not to infringe the patent, the 'close copy' products born of molecular roulette. Dr Alan Klass has observed:

> The time-lag factor is of such duration that by the time a new drug is proven to cause serious adverse side effects, it will have already justified itself financially to the manufacturer. Although certainly not purposely created by the drug firm, time-lag is an important element reducing the financial risk of introducing new drugs.[25]

The avoidance of drug disasters depends in part, then, on the efficient monitoring of drugs after they are in use. In 1966 the World Health Organisation inaugurated a pilot project of drug-monitoring on an international scale, and in 1971 a Research Centre was set up at Geneva to carry on this job. National agencies co-operate and are in turn warned immediately of the experiences of other countries.

The most that we can reasonably ask *before* drugs are introduced is that they should be beneficial and should have been properly tested to find any *discoverable* risks. In this country responsibility for the efficacy and safety of new drugs has lain primarily with the manufacturer. As we have seen, Governments were more concerned over pharmaceutical prices than safety, until the thalidomide tragedy occurred. Only then was the need for intervention accepted here. Only then were controls made stricter in the United States, where Senator Paul Douglas of Illinois, commending the acceptance of a drug bill by the Senate in 1962, asked: 'Can we learn from this lesson, or can mankind educate itself only by disaster and tragedy?'[26]

Have we learned? Stricter regulations were introduced in most countries. The development of control in this country will be traced, and then, by way of comparison, that in the United States.

Regulation of pharmaceuticals

United Kingdom

The first law governing medicines in this country was passed in 1540. It allowed certain 'assessors' of the College of Physicians in London to enter any apothecary's shop, check the medicaments, and throw out any they judged to be unfit or impure. But in 1542 the 'Quack's Charter' was passed: anyone could treat wounds or disease by whatever herbs, roots or ointments they chose. Charlatans profited for a further three centuries.

The British Pharmacopoeia, establishing standards for the strength and purity of medicines, was first published in the 1860s. In 1875 the first Food and Drugs Act imposed penalties for the adulteration of drugs. The manufacture and import of biological substances such as vaccines, sera and insulin was regulated by the Therapeutic Substances Act 1925. A few statutes prohibited the advertising to the public of products which purported to help in the treatment of certain serious diseases, such as cancer, epilepsy, tuberculosis and venereal diseases. From 1920 onwards, when the Dangerous Drugs Act was passed, control was exercised over drugs of dependence like opium and cocaine.[27]

Amazingly, there was no law aimed at ensuring the safety of pharmaceutical products until 1968. As Professor Sir Eric Scowen, chairman of the Committee on Safety of Medicines, has said: 'Lulled into security by the quiet years, both public and government were unprepared for the therapeutic explosion of the last 30 years. This complacency was rudely shattered by the thalidomide tragedy'.[28]

At the time of the thalidomide tragedy any medicine, however inadequately tested, however dangerous, could be brought on to the market without any registration or licensing being necessary and without any independent body having to be satisfied of its safety. The Ministry of Health's only action came when a prescription for a new product first reached the pricing bureau. Then they requested information from the maufacturer on the medicine, especially clinical information, which was considered by the Committee on the Classification of Proprietary Pharmaceutical Products. This was a committee established with the inception of the National Health Service, to classify drugs for the benefit of doctors. The committee awarded the products one of five categories: 'N' (new drugs of proved value), 'S' (similar to standard pharmacopoeia preparations), 'P' (new drugs not yet fully proved), 'O' (of little of no value), or 'H' (mixtures of 'O' and other categories). In the three more favourable categories, new drugs were freely prescribable; if the category was unfavourable, there were restrictions on the frequency of prescription, but it was still prescribable. As a check on safety, the committee's influence was minimal. Thalidomide was classified as 'N'.

Following the tragedy of thalidomide, in July 1962 the annual meeting of the British Medical Association called for an independent organisation to supervise the introduction of new drugs. In the same month the

Minister of Health, Mr Enoch Powell, announced that the English and Scottish Standing Medical Advisory Committees were considering the situation. They set up a joint sub-committee under the chairmanship of Lord Cohen of Birkenhead, which produced an interim report in November and a final report in April 1963.[29] Considering that manufacturers had by and large acted responsibly 'within the limits of existing knowledge of methods of testing', the sub-committee found it neither desirable nor practicable to transfer responsibility for testing to a central authority. Instead, it recommended that manufacturers should continue to be responsible for laboratory testing, but that a central regulatory agency should be set up on a voluntary basis to review toxicity data of new drugs, and the results of clinical trials, and to collect reports from general practitioners and hospitals of adverse reactions to drugs in clinical use.

These recommendations were closely heeded by the Government, and led to the appointment by the Health Minister of the Committee on Safety of Drugs under the chairmanship of Sir Derrick Dunlop, which began work in 1964. The Dunlop Committee formed three sub-committees, corresponding to the stages of testing a new drug: one to check on toxicity tests done on animals, to ascertain the best formulation and dosage details and to study metabolism reports; one to study clinical trials; and one concerned with collection and analysis of details of adverse reactions appearing after a drug had been put on the market. No compulsion was involved, but manufacturers were invited to seek the approval of the Committee before introducing any new drugs. The pressure to do so was high since the National Health Service was the industry's chief customer, and since doctors could be warned that a drug had been marketed without the Committee's approval. The co-operation of all the major manufacturers was ensured when both the Association of the British Pharmaceutical Industry and the Proprietary Association of Great Britain promised that their members would not offer a drug for clinical trial, or market any new medicines, against the Committee's advice.

A manufacturer submitting a new drug for approval was obliged to provide suitable reports (typically running to several thousand pages) of experiments on animals and sometimes human volunteers, which should show the drug's mode of action, toxicity, efficacy, and chemical and physical properties. Because of the thalidomide tragedy, testing of the drug's effect on the foetuses of pregnant laboratory animals was expected. Once the Committee was satisfied from adequate information that the new substance was likely to be useful and safe, it would authorise the manufacturers to arrange clinical trials in an approved manner. The time involved and costs of developing a new drug were increased, as inevitably was the standard of care. When the pharmaceutical companies became aware of what the Committee's requirements, were submissions of new drugs (of which there were about sixty or seventy a year) could usually be handled in three or four months, while the hundreds which merely involved minor reformulations could be approved more quickly. The overall rate of submissions which were rejected, or withdrawn by the manufacturers, was about 10 per cent.[30]

For the monitoring of side effects, all prescribing doctors in the country (and hospitals, dentists, medical officers of health, coroners and the pharmaceutical industry) were (and still are) issued with a stock of yellow cards which they were asked to fill in and post to the Committee whenever they encountered an adverse reaction in a patient. These were sent in at a rate of between 3,000 and 4,000 per year. This figure compares favourably with the response of doctors in other countries to similar schemes. No doubt, as Sir Derrick Dunlop has pointed out, this was because: 'We are perhaps in a better position in Britain today than in any other country to estimate the extent of a medicine's use as all prescriptions written under the National Health Service become available for analysis'.[31] But the Committee continually appealed to doctors to report more often. When a yellow card was received, the details were fed into a computer which printed out a data sheet saying whether that drug or related drugs had previously produced a similar reaction. This information was then sent back to the notifying practitioner. Special investigations of particular drugs were also carried out. Perhaps the best-known example of the working of the system was the investigation undertaken in 1966 by the Committee – together with the Medical Research Council and the Royal College of General Practitioners – of the link between oral contraceptives and venous thrombosis, leading to the recommendation of the low oestrogen content pills as safer.

Public reaction to the thalidomide tragedy created an atmosphere in which doctors and the pharmaceutical industry were prepared to accept controls. The Dunlop Committee sought, and obtained, a high degree of co-operation from the industry. The resultant system was generally admired for its efficiency, economy and flexibility. But in its second annual report in 1965, the Committee said:

Whilst it appears to the Committee that in meeting their responsibilities for the safety of drugs they have not been hampered in any
way by lack of statutory powers, largely due to the co-operation of
the manufacturers, they believe that the arrangement ought to be

given permanence within the framework of legislation. They welcome the assurance of the Minister that the aim will be to maintain under the statutory provisions the scope for flexibility and the exercise of professional responsibility which their experience has shown to be necessary.

The majority of Lord Cohen's sub-committee had preferred immediate action to reassure the public, while acknowledging that legislation was 'urgently required'. Two dissenting pharmacist members had called for early compulsory legislation, and this was recommended again in 1967 by the (Sainsbury) Committee of Enquiry into the Relationship of the Pharmaceutical Industry with the National Health Service.

The result was the Medicines Act 1968, which provided for the legal control of various aspects of the manufacture, distribution, use, labelling, advertising and packaging of medicines, and replaced the informal Dunlop Committee by a licensing system to which manufacturers *must* submit new medicines for approval.

Under the Act the Ministers of Health and Agriculture (veterinary products are included in the legislation) are given the role of licensing authorities to issue licences governing the marketing, importation and manufacture of medicines. Certificates are required before manufacturers may undertake clinical trials, and licences before products can be marketed. Certificates are granted for a period of two years, and product licences are renewable after five years. In dealing with an application for a product licence, under s.19(1), the licensing authority is directed to take into consideration:

(a)   the safety of medicinal products of each description to which the application relates;
(b)   the efficacy of medicinal products of each such description for the purposes for which the products are proposed to be administered; and
(c)   the quality of medicinal products of each such description, according to the specification and the mathod or proposed method of manufacture . . .

But by section 19(2), a drug will not be considered inefficacious merely because other products perform the same function as well or better. So the Act does not require a new product to be *demonstrably more effective* than those already available, a standard advocated by some but sacrificed in favour of the doctor's hallowed freedom to prescribe.

The Ministers are given wide powers of regulation over advertisements for medicines and the issue of false or misleading advertisements is made an offence with a maximum penalty of two years' imprisonment and a fine.

The 1968 Act provided for the establishment of a general body called the Medicines Commission to advise the Ministers on the execution of their functions, and for the Ministers to establish specialist committees as well. At the moment there are three expert committees, the Committee on Safety of Medicines, a Veterinary Products Committee, and a Pharmacopoeia Commission which has the job of producing the British Pharmacopoeia, the official compendium of formulae for preparing medicinal compounds. These three committees report directly to the Minister, but the Medicines Commission can act as the court of appeal from their decisions.

The Medicines Commission must have at least eight members, appointed after consultation with the relevant professions and the pharmaceutical industry. Currently it has sixteen members, only one of whom is a general practitioner. The Commission was intended as the country's principal advisory body on the use of medicines in society, but still seems to be in search of ways to perform this role. Its last chairman, Sir Ronald Bodley Scott, described the Commission's broad remit as 'almost too broad',[32] and regretted the lack of funds for research projects he thought desirable. Through committees, it has produced some useful reports, for example concerning which medicines should be on general sale and which should be prescription-only. Apart from that, it functions only as an occasional adviser to the Health Ministers.

Role perception is less of a problem to the Committee on Safety of Medicines which replaced the Committee on Safety of Drugs in 1971. Little has been changed except for the committee's name. The old committee was transmuted *en bloc* to become the new committee, still under the chairmanship of Sir Eric Scowen. The new committee leant heavily on the operational experience of its predecessor.

Obtaining a licence from the Committee for a new product has now of course become mandatory. Technically the licence is granted by the Minister and an appeal from a refusal lies to the Commission, but so far the advice of the Committee has always been followed. Since 1970, the number of new pharmaceuticals rejected by the Committee has been higher. Between 10 and 15 per cent of applications for clinical trials certificates, and a similar proportion of product licences, are either refused or withdrawn. In 1974 the failure rates were 13·9 per cent and 13·3 per cent respectively. This proportion seems high in view of the expensive years of work which may be done on a product in the pre-marketing stage: companies claim that only one in 5,000 laboratory

116

compounds actually succeeds in the market, and that by the time a new drug begins it commercial life more than £5 million, and about six years, have been spent on its research and development. The industry has criticised the safety committee as over-cautious. Thus Dr Gordon Fryers, the managing director of Reckitt and Colman's pharmaceutical division, has commented: 'I don't really accept the amount of effort and data which have to be put in before you can do anything in the way of clinical trials. This is very destructive. It takes very large sums of money and holds up production for a very long time'.[33] An allied criticism which has been made is that the Committee's membership is too academic and lacks practical experience of the problems facing the drug industry. Fifteen of the safety committee, out of eighteen, are indeed professors. But caution is probably expected of the committee both in view of fears as to safety and lest it be alleged that National Health Service patients taking part in clinical trials are being used as experimental animals. Public expectations, embodied in the Medicines Act, are that everything possible will be done to ensure the safety of a drug. Professor Scowen has pointed out that this leaves his committee little room for manoeuvre, and has replied to critics:

> In any case, there are very few new drugs for which we can't afford to wait a while. If something like penicillin did turn up, or if we were asked to look at a possible cure for some presently incurable disease, then we would consider very carefully whether we could not cut some corners to get the thing through quickly.[34]

The pattern set by the Dunlop Committee, then, has been followed. Responsibility for testing remains with manufacturers, although the Committee on Safety of Medicines can arrange for independent testing when dissatisfied with the information they provide.

Controls over the marketing of new medicines have been successfully introduced and improved since the thalidomide tragedy. The nature of drug action is such that some effects, for example long-term carcinogenic dangers, are only practically discoverable after years of clinical use. No regulatory system will eliminate drug-induced disease, though sensible prescribing and use will lessen its incidence.

The Committee on Safety of Medicines has also taken over the function of monitoring reactions to the drugs in use. In 1974 it received 4,818 notifications, but in the annual report commented that 'the numbers . . . still only represent a small proportion of those which actually occur',[35] and Professor Scowen has suggested that both hospital doctors and general practitioners might still co-operate more. Three official volumes of edited and selected extracts from the register of adverse reactions compiled between 1964 and 1974 have been published, comprising more than nine hundred pages of close print. When it becomes evident that a particular drug merits closer investigation, the Committee's forty or fifty part time medical field-workers appointed throughout the country follow up the reports by interviewing the doctors concerned. The results are conveyed to practitioners by 'Dear Doctor' letters. A 'yellow peril' warning was issued in 1975 concerning *Eraldin* (practolol), a beta-blocking agent which was found sometimes to cause permanent serious eye and skin disorders. It had previously been approved for marketing by the Committee. ICI, who made it, claimed that actions brought against them would be unsuccessful in view of their rigorous testing and the unforeseeability of long term side effects. They have however already paid out over £150,000 by way of compensation to those patients who suffered permanent damage and it is estimated that the overall cost may reach £1 million when all outstanding claims have been settled.[36]

When the Act came into force, product licences were granted as of right upon application by manufacturers in respect of their existing products. In November 1975 the Government announced the membership of a Committee on the Review of Medicines, to be chaired by Sir Eric Scowen, which will now begin to review the safety of the 36,000 or so products concerned by the same standards to which new drugs are now subject.

United States

At first sight is seems paradoxical that it is in the United States, traditionally committed to a *laissez-faire* philosophy, that governmental regulation of pharmaceuticals has been most comprehensive. But the excesses of freedom have their price, albeit unwillingly paid. A historian with a penchant for alliteration has described food and drug legislative history in America as composed of these principal features: 'change, complexity, competition, crusading, compromise, catastrophe'.[37]

'Change' connoted the beginnings of the revolution in science and technology. Its dimensions and complexity ensured that any measure would be of the omnibus kind, and typically legislative coverage has encompassed food and drink and drugs, and sometimes patent medicines and cosmetics.

It was the widespread adulteration of foodstuffs, spirits and medicinal drugs in the late nineteenth century that first caused the demand for legal intervention. Reputable farmers and processors resented the competition of the unscrupulous. A crusading Bureau of Chemistry chief at the Department of Agriculture, Harvey Washington Wiley, pressed for

118

legislation. Campaigning journalists disclosed the scandals of debased foods, unclean meat and dangerous nostrums. But business interests succeeded in delaying and modifying proposed legislation. Public pressure was brought to bear sufficiently on Congress only after Upton Sinclair, in his novel *The Jungle*, writing about the lives of immigrant workers in the packing houses, incidentally revealed the filthy conditions under which meat was being processed. A meat inspection amendment was rushed through Congress and the Pure Food and Drugs Act of 1906 was passed. It was aimed primarily at preventing adulteration, but also prohibited false or misleading labels on pharmaceuticals.

A quarter of a century later the discovery of the first sulphonamides had set the drug companies off on the search for powerful new drugs. It was in this transitional stage of the pharmaceutical revolution that the next protracted legislative battles were fought, which led to the 1938 Food, Drug and Cosmetic Act. The first draft of the new law was written by officials of the Food and Drug Administration (which had been formally established in 1931), who sought to close the loopholes in the existing law and give the consumer more protection. Consumer groups and national women's organisations were the pressure groups fighting hardest for the new law, but Walter Campbell, the chief of the FDA, recognised the need to compromise with the many trade associations involved. Tragedy proved to be the necessary catalyst for more stringent regulation: the death of 107 persons, many of them children, after ingesting the drug *Elixir of Sulfanilamide*. The Massengill Company's chief chemist had used a deadly poison as a solvent in its preparation. The company had distributed the medicine without having done any toxicity testing, conduct that was perfectly legal under the 1906 Act. The FDA was able to impound the product only on the ground of misbranding, since 'Elixir' wrongly implied that the preparation contained alcohol.

The Federal Food, Drug and Cosmetic Act[38] gave government the new role of prior evaluation of a drug's safety. Manufacturers were required to demonstrate the safety of new drugs to the FDA before they would be allowed to introduce them into interstate commerce[39]; clinical, chemical and manufacturing data about the drug had to be submitted; if the government took no negative action within 60 days of the application, it was deemed approved (the Secretary of Health, Education and Welfare could extend the period to 180 days if he thought it necessary). If the safety of a drug was questioned after marketing, the FDA were given powers to investigate and the Secretary of Agriculture was empowered to remove drugs from interstate commerce if they were found to be 'dangerous to health when used in the dosage or with

119

the frequency or duration prescribed, recommended, or suggested in the labelling thereof'.[40] By compelling manufacturers to strengthen their scientific staffs, the new laws encouraged more scientific methods; the former Commissioner of the FDA, George P. Larrick, has claimed that the 1938 Act was a major accelerating force in the discovery of new drugs.

Although an improvement over previous legislation, the 1938 Act proved to have weaknesses in practice, the effects of which became the more dangerous as powerful new medicines were introduced.[41] The FDA had only a limited time to find cause for rejecting an application on grounds of safety before it was automatically approved. Senator Kefauver, who was to propose a new law, observed that in 'so critical an area as drug safety, no automatic clearance should be possible, theoretically or in practice'.[42] The 1938 Act failed to provide for the monitoring of new drugs after they had been approved, or the systematic reporting of side effects. Yet the FDA's power to remove a drug from the market was hedged with restrictions, precluding immediate action except in cases of true disaster. The FDA had no power to conduct inspections of manufacturing plants. A manufacturer was not obliged to show that a new product was effective as well as safe. The advertising of prescription drugs was virtually unregulated.

A thalidomide disaster in America was prevented[43] not so much by the formal provisions of the 1938 Act or the policy of the FDA as by the stubbornness of a single medical officer. *Kevadon* (thalidomide) was Dr Frances Kelsey's very first new drug application. Suspicious of the inadequate data provided by Richardson-Merrell and alerted to the neuritis risk by a chance reading of the *British Medical Journal*, Dr Kelsey caused approval to be withheld on the ground that the application was incomplete. Pressure on her was intensified by Merrell representatives, who contacted her office more than fifty times, hinted that she had libelled them, and threatened to go to the Commissioner himself. Her refusal to give in prevented thousands of deformities; it earned her the nation's highest award for distinguished federal civilian service. The FDA leaders at the time, on the other hand, have been criticised for failing to shield Dr Kelsey from pressure and for failing to order a withdrawal of the samples of the drug already distributed to doctors. (Instead Commissioner Larrick asked the manufacturer to withdraw it, and thought that 'the firm proceeded with reasonable diligence'.)[44] Dr Helen Taussig, an American paediatrician who investigated the thalidomide disaster in Europe, wrote that the failure of *Kevadon* to reach the American market was 'because of a lucky combination of circumstances . . . [and Dr Kelsey's alertness] . . . not because of the existence of any legal requirement that the drug might have failed to meet'.[45] A large question-mark hangs over the working of the FDA at this period, for in 1960 Dr Barbara Moulton, who had worked as a drug examiner with the agency for five years, testified before a Senate sub-committee that she had resigned: 'because the Food and Drug Administration had failed utterly in its solemn task of enforcing those sections of the law dealing with the safety and misbranding of drugs, particularly prescription drugs'.[46] Thalidomide, the might-have-been disaster so narrowly avoided, was the spur for further legislation.

This time, the crusade was led from within Congress. In 1957 the late Estes Kefauver, a Democratic Senator from Tennessee, had taken over as the new chairman of the Senate Sub-committee on Antitrust and Monopoly. Kefauver was a progressive intellectual who had made antitrust matters his speciality. His staff included two economists, John Blair and Irene Till, who became increasingly interested in the high price of pharmaceuticals, and part of the Sub-committee's staff was assigned to a preliminary investigation of the drug industry.

Preliminary inquiries suggested that the industry was surprisingly uncompetitive. There was found to be a close identity of prices, with price leadership by the bigger firms. Doctors mostly prescribed brand name drugs advertised by the big firms even when the same drug was produced much more cheaply by a small concern or on a generic name basis. The breakthrough came with the discovery that the Schering Corporation could profitably sell prednisone to the Military Medical Supply Agency at $23·63 a bottle when it was sold to the commercial trade for $170 per bottle. Subpoenas went out to nineteen major drug companies ordering submission of patient-licensing agreements and purchase-and-sale contracts. When these were received, enormous disparities between production costs and sale prices were revealed; often the mark-up was more than a thousand per cent.

Kefauver had been under pressure to drop the drug investigation, a political hot potato, but decided that the evidence of excessive prices and profits was too serious to ignore. In December 1959 he began chairing investigative hearings on the drug industry.

First there were hearings on some specific products – the cortical steroids, tranquillisers, oral antidiabetics and antibiotics. Later the Sub-committee heard evidence on more general issues. The picture of excessive profits suggested by earlier investigation was confirmed. Kefauver, cross-examining spokesmen for the drug firms, repeatedly faced them with the huge mark-ups on their products, which they could attempt to justify only by elaborating the costs of promotion and distribution (amounts which were themselves open to attack) and by frequent incantation of

121

'research costs'. But much of what passed as research was shown to be mere molecular manipulation with the aim of modifying the original drug just enough to get a patentable derivative. The drug firms pointed to the large number of research failures they had for every success. But Dr A. D. Console, who had been Squibb's medical director for five years, testified on that point:

> This is true, since it is the very essence of research. The problem arises out of the fact that they market so many of their failures ... And I should point out that with many of these products it is clear while they are on the drawing board that they promise no utility. They promise sales.[47]

The initial impetus for the hearing had been high prices. But gradually all aspects of the practices and ethics of the pharmaceutical industry came under scrutiny and often there was the smell of something rotten, such as abuse of the patent system, concealment of side effects, or aggressive and misleading advertising.

Kefauver's response was to draft a bill which he submitted to the Senate on 12 April 1961. His aims were primarily to lower drug prices, to increase competition and to protect the consumer. The protracted struggle which ensued is documented step-by-step in Richard Harris's *The Real Voice*, which offers a fascinating, if to British eyes disquieting, insight into the American legislative process. The bill seemed likely to founder on the hostility of conservative Senators, or at the least to be emasculated. President Kennedy promised in his 1962 State of the Union Message, 'To protect our consumers from the careless and the unscrupulous, I shall recommend improvements in the food and drug laws'. But the administration was generally ambivalent in its attitude. Through Representative Oren Harris it introduced a weaker drug bill into the House of Representatives, and some of the President's men – representatives of the Department of Health, Education and Welfare, now responsible for the FDA – met secretly behind Kefauver's back with the staff men of some of the other Senators on the Antitrust Sub-committee to agree on a watered-down version of Kefauver's bill. While the secret meeting was bitterly denounced by Kefauver in the Senate, *The Washington Post* reported on thalidomide under the heading 'Heroine of FDA Keeps Bad Drug off Market', and shortly there were indications from the President that the weakened Senate bill did not, after all, go far enough to protect the consumer. The text of amendments suggested by the President soon followed, and a bill based on them was later passed unanimously in the Senate. The Harris bill went through the House of Representatives, and both bills then went to

122

the Senate—House Conference for the differences to be ironed out. Richard Harris has suggested that 'the bill that [came] out of conference was, in sum, stronger than either of those that had gone in'.[48]

The Kefauver—Harris Amendments[49] (to the 1938 legislation) were signed by President Kennedy on 10 October 1962. The powers, and the responsibility, of the FDA are greatly increased.[50]

Thus the FDA is given discretionary power over a manufacturer's clinical research stage. Prior to any tests on humans, manufacturers now have to submit a new drug investigational plan giving the animal testing results and the scheme proposed for human tests. The FDA's evaluation may lead it to prohibit or delay clinical research which appears unduly risky or does not follow sound scientific procedures.

The FDA's power to control the release of drugs on the market is expanded by Section 102, whereby manufacturers are required to show that their drugs are safe and effective. A new drug application may be denied, or an approved drug withdrawn, if the requisite tests 'do not show that such drug is safe for use' or when 'there is a lack of substantial evidence that the drug will have the effect it purports or is represented to have'. Drugs may also be summarily withdrawn from the market if they present 'an imminent hazard to the public health'.

Tighter standards are established for assessing safety and effectiveness. For example it is provided that approval of a new drug for marketing may be denied if the manufacturer's research reports are inconclusive or if proposed labelling is 'false or misleading in any particular'. And the FDA is empowered to review information other than that provided by the drug company in deciding. The marketing of all antibiotics for human use was made subject to batch-by-batch certification of their safety, quality and strength.[51]

Section 104 of the Amendments removes the possibility of automatic clearance of new drug applications. It provides that an application is not passed until the FDA has affirmatively determined the effectiveness and safety of the new drug and has so notified the applicant. The Secretary of Health, Education and Welfare has 180 days (or additional time, if agreed) after the application is filed and must then either affirmatively approve it or give the applicant notice of opportunity for a hearing at which to contest lack of approval. The hearing, if requested, must commence within a further 120 days. Presumably these time limits are intended to give sufficient time for assessment while ensuring also that the introduction of useful drugs is not delayed through bureaucratic inertia.

Under the 1938 legislation the drug companies were not obliged to furnish the FDA with any information on side effects or clinical experience after a new drug had been approved for marketing, and the FDA itself lacked the resources to monitor drugs for later harmful effects. Section 103 of the Amendments empowers the Secretary to require manufacturers to maintain such records relating to clinical experience and other data or information which would assist in the continuing evaluation of the drug's effectiveness and safety. Section 103 also lays down much stricter legal control over applications from manufacturers to begin experimental clinical use of drugs, in particular by requiring adequate pre-clinical studies.

Every drug producer is required to register annually with the Secretary. His plant must be operated in conformity with 'current good manufacturing practice', and FDA inspectors may inspect both establishment and records.

Section 111 of the Amendments authorises the Secretary in certain circumstances to determine an official name for a drug in the interest of 'achieving usefulness and simplicity'. This provision was inserted because some drug companies have allegedly tried to choose tongue-twisting, unmemorable generic names so as to encourage brand name prescribing. Section 112 further provides that the official or generic name must appear in print at least half as large as the brand name wherever the latter is used in advertising or labelling. There are new provisions on prescription drug advertising reflecting public disquiet and lack of optimism about the willingness of the medical profession and pharmaceutical industry to put their own houses in order. Section 131 gives the FDA the responsibility of providing by regulations that all advertising materials should contain a 'brief summary relating to side-effects, contraindications and effectiveness'. These regulations have now been made and the key concept is that a 'fair balance' of information must be presented.

Conclusion

The 1962 Amendments and regulations made under them give the United States comprehensive control over drug safety *to the extent that such control is practical*. Since 1962 the FDA have adopted a very cautious attitude to new drugs.

In fact there have been suggestions that legal requirements are too stringent. Professor David Cavers has warned:

> . . . in this field of professional activity where the law's relations with medicine and science are so uneasy, all three callings will have to maintain a continuing scrutiny of the operation and effects of

governmental controls if the effort to reinforce ethical obligations by legal duties is not to impair the progress of research and innovation in drug therapy.[52]

Taking up this theme in a recent study, *Regulation and Drug Development*,[53] Dr William Wardell and Dr Louis Lasagna argue that innovation has been inhibited. The cost of introducing a new drug has jumped from an average of $1·3 million in 1968 to $10·5 million in 1975, they find. They also show that of 180 new drugs introduced in both Britain and the United States in 1962–71, only 21 were first available in America.

However, all that this convincingly shows is that the time-lag in America is greater. Arguably, the cost of this is that patients are unnecessarily denied for a year or so the relief from suffering that a new drug might bring. But the FDA Commissioner, Alexander Schmidt, while conceding that there is a time-lag, has maintained: 'There have been no significant therapeutic breakthroughs in other countries that this country has gone without'.[54] He might also have added that the two examples of significant differences between the United Kingdom and the United States in recent years have been the hundreds of thalidomide victims and the thousands of deaths from the use of aerosols for asthma in the former. Obviously, more permissive systems have their cost too, and it seems a greater one. In a macabre way, the United States benefits from the public in other countries being used in a guinea-pig manner. Though the regulations governing pharmaceutical products in the two countries look similar on paper, the stronger effectiveness requirement in America, and the more repressive spirit in which the controls are applied, seem to have been amply justified.

Law has a role to play in drug safety, but social factors are important too. There was a salutary reminder of this in 1975 when it was found that use of some hormone drugs to test pregnancy involved a risk of deforming the foetus. Dr. C.N. Brown, who had been medical director of DCBL, wrote to *The Sunday Times*:

> I had hoped that the bitter experience of thalidomide would serve at least one useful purpose and that people, especially *women of child-bearing age*, would avoid the unnecessary use of powerful and potentially damaging agents . . .
> Will they never learn?[55]

Notes

[1] Cited in P. Talalay, (ed.), *Drugs in Our Society*, Johns Hopkins Press 1964, p.223.

[2] Figures from A. Klass, *There's Gold in Them Thar Pills*, Penguin 1975, p.155.

[3] Figures from *The Pharmaceutical Industry and the Nation's Health*: a booklet issued by the Association of the British Pharmaceutical Industry 1972.

[4] Central Statistical Office, *Social Trends*, HMSO 1974.

[5] J. Powles, 'On the Limitations of Modern Medicine', *Science, Medicine and Man*, vol.1, no.1, April 1973, p.1.

[6] See, for example, in praise: F.H. Happold, *Medicine at Risk*, Queen Anne Press 1967 and W. Breckon, *The Drug Makers*, Eyre Methuen 1972. In denigration: V. Coleman, *The Medicine Men*, Temple Smith 1975 and A. Malleson, *Need Your Doctor Be So Useless?*, Allen and Unwin 1973.

[7] F.H. Happold, *Medicine at Risk*, p.16 and p.205.

[8] *The Times* 7 June 1976.

[9] Quoted in M. Muller, 'Drug Companies and the Third World', *New Scientist*, vol.70, no.998, April 1976, p.216.

[10] See Monopolies Commission report, *Chlordiazepoxide and Diazepam*, HMSO 1973.

[11] See M.H. Cooper, *Prices and Profits in the Pharmaceutical Industry*, Pergamon 1965 and *International Price Comparison*, NEDO 1972.

[12] *Pfizer Corporation* v. *Ministry of Health* [1965] A.C.512.

[13] Report of the Committee of Enquiry into the Relationship of the Pharmaceutical Industry with the National Health Service 1965–67, HMSO 1967, Cmnd. 3410.

[14] *The Pharmaceutical Industry and the Nation's Health*, 1976, p.4.

[15] *The Times* 14 May 1976.

[16] *Focus on Pharmaceuticals*, HMSO 1972, p.31.

[17] *The Times (Europa)* 2 April 1974. In France, for example, there were more than 2,000 pharmaceutical firms in 1950 and there are fewer than 400 now.

[18] See P.D. Rheingold, 'The MER/29 Story – An Instance of Successful Mass Disaster Litigation', *California Law Review*, vol.56, 1968, p.116.

[19] Quoted in W. Breckon, *The Drug Makers*, p.121.

[20] See A. Norton, *Drugs, Science and Society*, Fontana 1973, ch.3.

[21] See W.H.W. Inman and A.M. Adelstein, 'Rise and Fall of Asthma Mortality in England and Wales in Relation to Use of Pressurised Aerosols', *The Lancet*, vol.2, 1969, p.279.

[22] See P.F. D'Arcy and J.P. Griffin, *Iatrogenic Diseases*, Oxford 1972.

[23] D.R. Laurence, *Clinical Pharmacology*, Churchill (3rd ed.), 1966.

[24] See V. Coleman, *The Medicine Men*, pp.80–8.

[25] A. Klass, *There's Gold in Them Thar Pills*, p.127.

[26] Quoted in R. Harris, *The Real Voice*, Macmillan 1964, p.215.

[27] See H. Teff, *Drugs, Society and the Law*, Saxon House 1975, ch.2.

[28] *Financial Times* 10 August 1971.

[29] Safety of Drugs, HMSO 1963.

[30] Figures from the Annual Reports of the Committee on Safety of Drugs, HMSO.

[31] Quoted in V. Coleman, *The Medicine Men*, p.131.

[32] Quoted in D. Gould, 'Can We Handle Modern Drugs?', *New Scientist*, 23 May 1974, pp.460–1.

[33] Ibid., p.463.

[34] Ibid., p.464.

[35] Annual Report for 1974 of the Medicines Commission, HMSO 1975.

[36] *The Times* 12 July 1976.

[37] J.H. Young, 'Social History of American Drug Legislation' in P. Talalay (ed.), *Drugs in Our Society*, p.217.

[38] Act of June 25, 1938, ch.675.

[39] Ibid., s.505.

[40] Ibid., s.502(j).

[41] See J.M. Pisani, 'Drug Safety and the FDA', *Food Drug Cosmetic Law Journal*, vol.21, 1966, p.68.

[42] 108 Cong. Rec. 14681.

[43] Ten thalidomide babies were born in the United States, because experimental use of the drug prior to marketing was permitted at the time and more than two million tablets had been distributed to doctors as free samples. See M. Mintz, *The Therapeutic Nightmare*, ch.12.

[44] In evidence to Senator Humphrey's Sub-committee on Reorganisation and International Organisation. Quoted in R. Harris, *The Real Voice*, p.193.

[45] H. Taussig article in *Scientific American*, August 1962.

[46] Quoted in R. Harris, *The Real Voice*, p. 106. See also J. Lear, 'The Unfinished Story of Thalidomide', *Saturday Review*, 1 September 1962.

[47] Ibid., p.78.

[48] Ibid., p.240.

[49] Act of October 10, 1962, Public Law 87–781.

[50] See generally P.D. Rheingold, 'Products Liability – The Ethical Drug Manufacturer's Liability', *Rutgers Law Review*, vol.18, 1964, p.947.

[51] S.105.

[52] D.F. Cavers, 'The Legal Control of the Clinical Investigation of

Drugs' in P.A. Freund (ed.), *Experimentation with Human Subjects*, Allen and Unwin 1972, p.242.

[53] W. Wardell and L. Lasagna, *Regulation and Drug Development*, American Enterprise Institute, 1975.

[54] *Time* 29 September 1975.

[55] *The Sunday Times* 8 June 1975.

5 Reforming the system

Despite the introduction of new controls and safety measures, one cannot rule out the possibility of another drug disaster comparable to thalidomide. Are we now in any better position to cope? Testing for effects on the foetus has become standard practice and the law has put beyond doubt the right of the unborn child to sue. But foetal deformity is only one way in which drugs may cause injury. It is also salutary to remember how dependent the children's claims were on non-legal factors such as the *Sunday Times* campaign and the attitude of institutional investors.

The legal significance of the thalidomide litigation stretches far beyond its particular facts. It has highlighted some fundamental shortcomings of the tort system and, as a result of the massive publicity which it attracted, has paved the way for change, and proposals for change, on an almost unprecedented scale. What are the broader legal issues which it brings into focus, and how can the deficiencies it has exposed be remedied?

Criticism of the system may be levelled on two distinct but related grounds: the fact that the consumer has to prove negligence to succeed against the manufacturer, and the defects of the procedural framework within which the parties operate. Dissatisfaction on both scores has led some countries to explore other means of compensating the victims of defective products. Though differing on points of detail, these approaches are reducible to two basic models: the imposition of strict liability on the manufacturer, or the substitution of a comprehensive system of state insurance. In neither case does the injured party have the burden of proving anyone's negligence. Before we examine these alternatives, we need to examine a little more closely why negligence is increasingly felt to be an inadequate basis of liability.

The weaknesses of fault liability

The thalidomide dispute is a microcosm of much that is wrong with negligence liability as a mechanism for compensating accident victims. But it is only one specific, and in certain key respects unique, instance of injury resulting from defective products. The whole field of defective products itself covers only a small fraction of personal injury actions, of which some 90 per cent are accounted for by road accident cases and injuries sustained at work. These in turn represent only a small proportion of total incapacity, when one takes account of accidents in the home, illness and congenital disability. To see the problem of reforming English law on liability for defective products in perspective, we need to consider, however briefly, the existing framework of tort compensation and entitlement to state benefits, and the relation between them.[1]

The victim of any injury amounting to negligence in law is entitled to tort damages, always assuming that he can prove the fault of another party. If the injury occurs while he is in the course of employment, he is also, without having to prove fault, entitled to industrial injuries benefit·under the National Insurance (Industrial Injuries) Acts. If the accident does not occur in the course of employment, he would, in addition to his tort award, be able to claim social security benefits (for sickness and unemployment), provided he has paid his national insurance contributions. In either case there will be an element of overlapping compensation, since only half of the benefits for a period of five years are deducted from a tort award. Many other forms of double compensation can occur, since private insurance, pensions, charitable gifts and certain other benefits are not taken into account.

In appropriate circumstances, the state also provides supplementary benefits, compensation for the victims of violent crime, and a whole range of health, social and welfare services available according to the criterion of *need*, not *fault*. National insurance benefits are not comparable in amount to what may be obtained in a successful tort action because the latter provides for non-pecuniary loss. On the other hand, the introduction of earnings-related benefits has narrowed the gap and further called into question the utility of a separate tort system.

It is clear then that there is a multiplicity of available mechanisms for compensating the victims of personal injury, many of which already coexist in our society. Should we retain the negligence action in its present form, or modify it, for example by shifting the burden of proof on to the defendant? Should we replace it by a strict liability tort system, or by a state insurance scheme? Within these broad frameworks, a whole host of permutations present themselves. Several American and Canadian states have what are called 'no-fault' insurance laws, providing compensation regardless of fault, in the case of road traffic accidents only, as an *alternative* to negligence liability. Some of these schemes are run by private insurance companies, others by the state; some are voluntary, others are compulsory.[2] New Zealand has a comprehensive administrative system for compensating *all* accident victims.

130

One can perhaps best approach the problem of choosing between the various options by a process of exclusion. As a first step, and whether comprehensive or piecemeal solutions are to be preferred, we would argue for the abolition of the common law negligence action. As presently constituted it is inadequate and no amount of tinkering with it is likely to produce sufficient improvement to justify its retention. The supposed merits of negligence liability may be summarised as follows. It provides for detailed analysis of individual cases in a way not possible under a more mechanical administrative procedure; it contains an element of deterrence, and accords with most people's moral expectations, in that the person responsible for the injury is required to pay. Further, by permitting the ordinary citizen to initiate an action, it may serve to call wrongdoers to account through the sanction of adverse publicity, prevent the abuse of private or public power and pave the way for social reform.

On closer inspection, these arguments are not very convincing. Elaborate individual treatment is reserved for the minute proportion of accident cases which are not settled, and even in these the injured person's prospects of success will largely depend on the fortuitous circumstance of his being able to prove that the other party caused the accident and was at fault in doing so. In many road accidents, for example, witnesses are either non-existent or unwilling to become involved. Considerations of expense, delay and need will deter many victims from pursuing a remedy beyond any initial offer that is made.

The supposed deterrent effect of a tort action is often more illusory than real. We are after all talking about 'accidents', which by definition often just happen. In the bulk of road accidents and injuries at work, momentary inadvertence is more common than seriously culpable conduct and those concerned are aware that they are covered by insurance. The average motorist drives carefully to avoid death or injury. In so far as the law does provide an additional deterrent that impinges on his consciousness while he is driving, it is first and foremost the fear of a criminal conviction and only secondarily the thought that he might lose his no-claims bonus or incur an increase in his premium.

The alleged moral nature of fault liability has been seriously undermined in various ways. It is an insurance company which normally pays. The degree of fault involved may be minimal, taking little account of the particular characteristics of the defendant – a learner-driver, for example, is expected to exercise the same care as 'the competent and experienced driver'.[3] Above all, the amount of damages payable bears no relation to the degree of blameworthiness, being calculated according to the plaintiff's circumstances, primarily his loss of income, and is partly dictated in any case by constraints inherent in the machinery of negotiations with insurance companies.

There is perhaps more force in the notion of tort law as an instrument of social pressure. This theme has been explored by A.M. Linden, a leading Canadian tort lawyer, in his article, 'Tort Law as Ombudsman'.[4] It is interesting that he cites the thalidomide litigation in Canada as an example:

> Another way in which negative publicity causes financial loss is through diminution in the value of corporate shares. For example, when Richardson-Merrell, the producer of thalidomide and Mer/29, was sued by hundreds of people injured by these products, the value of its stock, which had been selling at twenty-five to thirty-five times its earnings, plunged to fifteen to twenty times its earnings. The shareholders suffered enormous financial losses, largely because investors feared that the numerous law suits against the company might bankrupt it.[5]

And again:

> What has happened in the field of products liability is worth examining in this context. Ordinary citizens have rendered accountable many manufacturers of shoddy goods, particularly in the United States, where thousands of tort suits are brought every year. For example, as a result of tort litigation, the producers of the thalidomide drug paid millions of dollars to the children their drug deformed. Although most claims never actually came to a trial on the merits, there was much public discussion of them. Many of the executive officers of the company had to spend many hours examining their practices, engaging in discussions with lawyers, and justifying their stewardship to their shareholders. It was tort law, not the administrative or the criminal process, that challenged the conduct of the drug company.[6]

But we are dealing here with a case that attracted an exceptional amount of publicity. The force of this argument is dependent on there being adverse publicity which will make some impact. It is also stronger in legal systems where a plaintiff's threat to sue is not an idle or half-hearted one. The development of tort principles through the cases in America is partially due to the existence of the contingent fee system, not permitted in England, under which lawyers receive a percentage of their clients' damages if they win, often about 30 per cent, and nothing if they lose.

132

The common law negligence action then provides only an elaborate process for compensating the few who achieve success in what Ison has aptly described as 'the forensic lottery'.[7]

For good measure, the tort system is very expensive to run. Various estimates suggest that on average at least 40 per cent of insurance premiums is absorbed in administrative costs. By comparison, the social security systems cost approximately 10 per cent of the total amounts paid out.[8] Could the existing defects be overcome without abandoning the tort framework, simply by introducing a system of strict liability, thereby relieving the plaintiff of the need to prove negligence?

Products liability: the American approach[9]

Its development and justification

The movement towards increased consumer protection is one of the more conspicuous developments of modern legal systems. The position of the consumer was formerly not distinguished from that of any other contractual party. Consequently, rules of contract law established in the main in the nineteenth century economic climate of *laissez-faire*, and more suited to the kind of commercial transaction where the parties are at arm's length, were applied indifferently to consumer sales. In Britain the law now acknowledges the consumer's relative lack of bargaining power in an age of monopolies and mass-produced goods. We have statutory recognition of the 'consumer' in the Supply of Goods (Implied Terms) Act 1973,[10] which restricts the seller's right to exclude or limit his liability in 'consumer sales'. Also, under the Fair Trading Act 1973, the Director-General of Fair Trading has the right to apply for an injunction against manufacturers who consistently produce substandard goods. But neither of these provisions will avail a consumer who wishes to sue the manufacturer. To do this, it is still necessary to prove negligence.

Many American states, while retaining the negligence action, have introduced additional remedies more in accord with the social and economic implications of modern marketing. One method has been to impose liability on the manufacturer for an express or implied breach of warranty. Originally this was a tort action based on the simple proposition that when a seller warranted the soundness or quality of goods which he put on the market, he should be held liable if they cause injury due to a defect, even if he was unaware of it. With the development of the law of contract, warranties came to be regarded as contractual obligations, which could exist only where there was an intention to contract. English law has therefore confined this kind of action to parties making a contract directly with one another, such as a retailer and his customer. But in the United States there is a wealth of case law and legislation[11] imposing such liability on manufacturers in favour of the ultimate consumer.

Though this approach may have worked in individual cases, it is far from ideal from a technical point of view, because it stretches the notion of contract artificially. It is particularly unsatisfactory in the context of prescription drugs where, strictly speaking, there is no 'sale' to the patient. The same difficulty arises with free hospital treatment, blood transfusions[12] and public vaccination programmes which go wrong. Weaknesses of this kind, coupled with a belief that social and economic policy, rather than the narrower notion of a contractual promise, justify holding the manufacturer responsible, eventually led many American states to adopt a strict liability doctrine in tort,[13] known as products liability. Provided the product is shown to be defective when it left him, the manufacturer is liable to the consumer even in the absence of negligence.

It is interesting to note that this development took place in common law jurisdictions where the law of torts is based on English law and is substantially the same in all other major respects. What inspired it? Apart from misgivings about the negligence action, perhaps the three justifications most commonly put forward are deterrence, moral responsibility and a rational allocation of risks.

The deterrence argument is in essence the popular idea that the stricter the liability to which he is subject, the more regard the manufacturer will pay to safety precautions. Another rationale is that he has a moral responsibility to stand behind his products. Through advertising he tries to persuade consumers in general to buy them and should foot the bill when things go wrong. In a free enterprise system, such liability may also be seen as the corollary of making profits when things go well. A less emotive approach would concentrate on the search for rational risk distribution. On this view, accident losses are an inevitable price of doing business and the manufacturer is normally able to calculate the risks more efficiently than the potential victim. Liability insurance and costing are brought out into the open, instead of being concealed within an apparently fault-based system.

However, the very process of labelling and separating these various rationales is rather artificial. It ignores the essentially pragmatic way in which many cases are decided and tends to convey an impression of mutually exclusive or competing explanations, when in reality they are frequently used to reinforce one another.[14] The deterrence argument, considered in isolation, is unconvincing. The change from negligence to products liability will provide only a minimal stimulus to safety in manufacture, since both systems are in practice underpinned by insurance. There is a more prosaic, yet more plausible explanation of safety levels than the fear of civil actions. Just as one drives safely in order to stay alive, so a company's production methods are largely dictated by its wish to survive and create goodwill, the ordinary controls implicit in running an effective business.

That there is a moral obligation to stand behind one's products seems incontrovertible, yet in certain respects it is less clearly applicable to pharmaceuticals than to industry in general. In the case of prescription drugs, the consumer/patient is to a large extent relying on the middle-man/doctor, for a product normally not advertised directly to the public. This necessarily complicates matters if one is stressing the moral responsibility of the producer; doubly so if, as with thalidomide, a foreign manufacturer grants a licence to distribute his product, while retaining a measure of control over sales promotion.

Nor is the currently popular risk distribution approach free from difficulty. If one takes as a starting point the proposition that for maximum efficiency the pharmaceutical industry should pay its own accident losses, several key issues are left in the air. What products are involved? If drugs only, how do we define 'drug'? If we extend liability to pharmaceutical products in general, is it feasible to work out a rational domestic form of risk-spreading when dealing with huge, multi-national, highly diversified concerns, which can vary their development, production and marketing methods so as to take advantage of the legal provisions, particularly tax laws, most favourable to them?

Problems of application to pharmaceuticals [15]

Even those American states most committed to products liability have encountered intractable legal problems with prescription drugs. Quite apart from the unique method of their distribution, the complex nature of the substances and their effects have posed problems of causation which far outweigh the difficulty of deciding whether the plaintiff lost his finger because of a faulty machine. Drugs are always potentially dangerous due to their toxicity. They are often taken by people who are already ill and who may be unusually susceptible to further ailments. Unlike many other products, they may cause injury in unpredictable ways, depending on the individual user's constitution. They may not be taken according to the instructions. The user may be allergic to a particular drug. Alternatively,

135

what appears to be an allergy may in fact be a toxic reaction. Presumably some balance has to be struck between a defence for the manufacturer based on allergy or idiosyncrasy and the competing tort principle that you take your victim as you find him.

The judicial dilemma was well expressed in a case decided in the Supreme Court of Oregon, *Cochrane* v. *Brooke* (1966).[16] The plaintiff suffered loss of vision after using *Chloroquine* for arthritis, because of an idiosyncrasy which made her unusually susceptible. Mr Justice Sloan observed:

> The far-reaching consequences that may ensue if we were to take so bold a step as to impose the absolute liability suggested by the plaintiff are beyond the ability of a court to know or comprehend. It is, indeed, easy for compassion to dictate an absolute liability against the makers of a product that can cause blindness. But once the liability is imposed, it could not be judicially limited only to cases involving disastrous consequences. An upset stomach caused by taking aspirin would, as well, entitle the user to his measure of damages. We can agree with the plaintiff that social justice might require that the price of the drugs should include an amount sufficient to create a fund to compensate those who suffer unanticipated harm from the use of a beneficial drug. But this kind of a system of compensation is beyond the power of a court to impose.

Many drugs, even when properly administered, produce harmful side effects, but are deemed medically acceptable because on balance their use is beneficial. This peculiarity has caused difficulties over the definition of *defect*, the hallmark of products liability. In Section 402A of the *Second Restatement of Torts*, a highly influential American work aimed at systematising the law of different states, defective products, for the purposes of strict liability, are confined to those which are '*unreasonably* dangerous', and this somewhat ambiguous formula has been adopted by a majority of states. An explanatory comment[17] on this provision shows that a product which is valuable yet unavoidably unsafe, such as rabies vaccine, would not be considered defective. Provided it is properly prepared and contains appropriate directions or warnings, it is not *unreasonably* dangerous.

The same argument is applied to many new or experimental drugs:

> ... as to which, because of lack of time and opportunity for sufficient medical experience, there can be no assurance of safety ...

but such experience as there is justifies the marketing and use of the drug notwithstanding a medically recognizable risk. The seller . . . is not to be held to strict liability . . . merely because he has undertaken to supply the public with an apparently useful and desirable product, attended with a known but apparently reasonable risk.[18]

If this is the general position with regard to 'known' risks, one would hardly expect it to be stricter when the risk was not scientifically discoverable at the time of marketing. In *Christofferson* v. *Kaiser Foundation Hospitals* (1971),[19] a woman's vision was irreversibly impaired, allegedly as a result of using *Aralen* to treat a skin ailment. The California District Court of Appeal held that Section 402A limits a drug manufacturer's duty to warn to situations where he 'has knowledge, or by the application of reasonable, developed human skill and foresight should have knowledge of . . . the danger'.[20] This principle was stated in general terms, though the particular case concerned an allergic reaction. Many states in fact do not impose strict liability even in the absence of warning of a known allergic reaction, unless a 'substantial' proportion of users would be affected by it. This qualification illustrates the priority attached by the courts to the overall benefits derived from particular drugs. In *Christofferson* v. *Kaiser Foundation Hospitals* the court emphasised the value of *Aralen* in treating serious ailments such as malaria. It is arguable that when safe substitutes exist a drug used to treat relatively minor conditions is '*unreasonably* dangerous', within the meaning of section 402A, even when the defect is wholly unforeseeable.

At all events, if strict liability is to be significantly different from negligence, it surely ought to apply in precisely those cases where the defendant is either not at fault, or the task of proving that he is lies beyond the resources of most litigants. But an underlying feature of the case law is the fear that too strict an approach would hinder new developments and put up costs. In several cases the fact that a *design* defect was scientifically undiscoverable at the time has been held to be a valid defence for the manufacturer. By contrast, a defect in the manufacturing *process* is felt to be one for which he ought to bear responsibility, as the price to be paid for his methods. Whether this is a tenable distinction is questionable, for the inevitability of allergic and other adverse drug reactions is as much a matter of common knowledge as the rogue product which slips through on the mass production line.

It has been suggested by Keeton[21] that manufacturers ought always to be strictly liable even in respect of unknowable risks of new drugs, where the harm outweighs the benefits. Others would go further and impose liability where an equally effective available drug would not have caused the injury.[22] Ehrenzweig[23] has proposed a 'typicality test', according to which there would be liability whenever the injury is broadly typical of the kinds of hazard to which the enterprise gives rise. No doubt there could be difficulties over the precise level of generality covered by such a test, but the basic notion is clear enough. Damage to the foetus resulting from the use of a particular drug, for example, may be completely unexpected, but should still import liability, being a side effect of a specifically medical character. One virtue of this approach is that it goes some way towards meeting the objection of the risk distribution school that where the risk is unknowable it is inappropriate to expect the manufacturer to insure against it.

A thalidomide victim would have had a greater prospect of success against the American distributors than against Distillers, at least in those states which take a strict view of manufacturer liability and permit a right of action on behalf of the non-viable foetus. This seems to be borne out by awards of over £300,000 in some cases, approximately six times those in most other countries, and high even by American standards. But, in general, strict liability is far from being absolute liability. There has been a marked reluctance to dispense entirely with fault notions, especially in the case of development risks. Strict liability and negligence, it has been said, are 'functionally interchangeable in most drug injury cases'.[24]

Products liability in Europe[25]

No European country has actually passed legislation imposing strict products liability on manufacturers as a general principle. France has developed the concept up to a point, through judicial interpretation, but most cases involve a fault requirement, however attenuated. In 1968, the Supreme Court of West Germany, in a case concerning vaccine for the inoculation of chickens,[26] established a strong presumption of manufacturer liability, reversing the normal rule that the plaintiff had the burden of proving the cause of the defect. In varying degrees other systems have relaxed the standard of proof demanded of the plaintiff. But as Prag notes in a comparative study of American, German and Scandinavian law on the subject,[27] in all these countries *development* defects have been treated as not creating products liability. At least where the manufacturer has shown the utmost care, damage due to an unknown

138

dangerous side effect has been considered an acceptable risk of everyday life.

However the discernible trend towards stricter liability has generated much activity of late, ranging from the investigations of our own Law Commission and the Pearson Commission to the deliberations of the Council of Europe and the European Economic Community. Because of increasing world trade in manufactured goods and the growth of multinational companies, the Council of Europe has been working towards a uniform approach in the interests of consumer protection. At the same time, a major concern of EEC members is that differing domestic laws on the extent and strictness of liability could distort competition through an unequal distribution of the insurance burden as between producers in different member states.

Whether in fact the cost of products liability insurance represents a sufficient proportion of overall costs to make a significant inroad into competition is open to doubt. Nor, to the extent that products are sold outside the Community, could harmonisation of the laws of *producer* countries within the Common Market achieve its purpose. For it will not normally be the law of the country where the producer is resident which applies. In the event of a dispute, each country's legal system has its own rules (of private international law) to determine the applicable law. The typical solution to the problem in the past has been that the law of the country where the injury occurs prevails. The most common alternative is to apply the law of the country in which the plaintiff habitually resides. Clearly the choice of law is of vital practical importance, as the conflict over jurisdiction in the Turkish Airlines DC-10 disaster – the world's biggest airline crash – strikingly demonstrated. Not only will the plaintiff's chances of proving his case often be greater under a system of law which provides remedies of the kind to be found in American jurisdictions, but the amounts recovered may differ enormously. As well as variations in the 'tariff' for particular injuries, countries have different laws on other aspects of compensation. Is the plaintiff entitled to an award if he has also received compensation from another source, such as private insurance? Will he receive anything at all for non-pecuniary loss?

Some tentative steps towards harmonisation of private international law rules in such matters have already been taken. The Hague Convention on the Law Applicable to Products Liability (1972) lays down rules of procedure to determine which country's laws should apply in the event of a dispute, though it has not as yet been ratified by any of its signatories.

Attempts are also currently being made to harmonise the *content* of national laws on defective products, along strict liability lines. A Council of Europe Draft Convention on Products Liability (1975)[28] has been submitted to the governments of member states. Should the United Kingdom decide to accede, its law will have to be altered to conform with the provisions of the Convention, though existing domestic law would remain in force to the extent that it was more favourable to the injured party.

Under the Draft Convention, the manufacturer of finished products (including an importer or licensee) would be liable as a 'producer'[29] to pay compensation for death or personal injuries caused by a defect. The injured person would have to establish the defect, the damage and the causal link between them. The producer would then be able to escape liability only if *he*[30] could prove that the defect did not exist when the product was put into circulation. But, significantly, 'development risks' presented the one area about which some misgivings were expressed. Though they are included, contracting states would be able to limit liability in respect of them.[31] This compromise was reached soon after the West German government's decision to establish a compensation fund to which all pharmaceutical manufacturers must contribute. A plaintiff unable to prove fault or enforce a judgement can have recourse to this fund for compensation up to a specified maximum amount.[32]

Early ratification of the Council of Europe Draft Convention is unlikely, partly because industrial interests may wait to see whether the final EEC proposals turn out to be more favourable to them. A Directorate of the Commission has produced a preliminary draft directive and explanatory memorandum (1974)[33] which, if adopted in anything resembling its present form, would necessitate changes in English law. The draft directive is also based on a strict liability approach, but is more favourable to producers in providing for an (as yet unspecified) limitation of liability for damages in *all* cases, and in expressly excluding compensation for non-pecuniary loss. However, it too would permit alternative domestic law remedies and all EEC countries allow compensation for such loss. Clearly, the possibility of resort to other remedies will to some extent undermine harmonisation. Indeed the very existence of two sets of parallel but mutually exclusive proposals, vying for the endorsement of European countries is hardly propitious. As Paul Storm, a Dutch advocate and a leading authority in the field, wrote in mid-1975: '... there is so much opposition to the drafts (especially from Germany and Italy where the industry lobby seems to be particularly strong) ... that within the next 10 years no such instrument is likely to come into force'.[34]

English developments

Whatever the eventual European outcome, the current focus on products liability is already having repercussions in England. The Law Commission is considering the adequacy of existing English law on defective products; while the Pearson Commission's broadly-based inquiry into compensation generally makes specific reference to 'death or personal injury (including ante-natal injury) suffered by any person . . . through the manufacture, supply or use of goods or services . . .'.

Under its terms of reference, the Law Commission has confined its analysis to remedies which are, or could be, available under a system based on litigation between the parties. But the Pearson Commission is in a position to make proposals to remove injury claims from the province of the courts altogether and replace them by some form of administrative scheme, perhaps along the lines of the one already functioning in New Zealand.

In a Working Paper, *Liability for Defective Products*,[35] the Law Commission has drawn attention to 'seven crucial questions'[36] which arise if a strict tort liability approach were to be adopted for personal injuries. Would it apply to the producer alone, or include others in the chain of distribution? How should 'defect' be defined? What products would be affected? What defences should be allowed? Should liability be limited to pecuniary losses? Should there be limits on the amount recoverable? Who should bear the burden of proof?

Several of these matters have already been raised, but further mention should be made of the range of possible defendants. Distillers, as it happens, manufactured as well as distributed thalidomide. We have concentrated on the position of the manufacturer not simply for this reason, but primarily because he is the most appropriate defendant in an action concerning defective goods based on negligence. Under a strict liability system one might wish to take account of the whole chain of production and distribution. Section 402A of the Second American Restatement, for example, applies not only to the producer, but also to the retailer and all other sellers in the chain. As the Law Commission points out, on grounds of consumer protection there is a strong case for making everyone involved in the marketing enterprise strictly liable to the consumer, leaving them to settle their claims against each other according to the terms of their respective contracts, or such rights of contribution as the law of torts allows. The plaintiff would not then be at risk because of chance factors such as the defendant being a foreign manufacturer or insolvent. But for consumers in general this would be a less advantageous form of risk distribution than confining strict liability to the producer and retaining the existing liability of others, since the extra cost of insurance cover would put up the price of goods.

The Commission specifically considers whether pharmaceuticals ought to be treated as a special case, 'particularly at the development stage'. 'It may be argued . . . that there are risks in new products that cannot be foreseen however careful the producer is, and that these are inevitable risks which the public must accept.'[37]

More comprehensive solutions

To the extent that they absolve the plaintiff from having to prove negligence, the strict liability solutions may be considered an improvement, even if, particularly for pharmaceuticals, the distinction is often more apparent than real. But unfortunately the weaknesses of a negligence approach are not confined to the difficulty of establishing the tort of negligence itself, but extend to the whole procedural framework which, under the schemes outlined above, would remain.

In Britain, court procedure compares unfavourably in many respects with, for example, the scheme for administering industrial injuries. The majority of industrial injury claims are adjudicated by an insurance officer on the basis of a medical certificate and evidence that the accident occurred in the course of employment. In addition to a six-month entitlement to a flat-rate weekly sum, with an earnings-related supplement, a disablement pension is payable for long term injuries. A medical board decides the extent of the disability, if satisfied that it was caused by the accident. Though the detailed rules on awards for particular disabilities are complex, at least their calculation is much more closely defined than in the common law system.

There are rights of appeal on medical and legal issues to tribunals, and from them to the Industrial Injuries Commissioner. Judicial review is minimal. The procedure in the appellate tribunals contrasts strikingly with the courts. The absence of an adversary approach, and for the most part of legal representation, makes for a more informal, less technical and speedier process. Moreover, the employer is required to investigate the circumstances of an accident and send in a report to the Department of Health and Social Security. As Atiyah concludes:

> It is hard to believe that anyone could make a dispassionate review of
> the tort system and the industrial injury system without coming to

the firm conclusion that on almost every count the latter is the superior and more up to date model of a compensation system.[38]

The New Zealand scheme[39]

If even the strict liability models would result in piecemeal reform, perhaps creating further anomalies without removing inherent weaknesses, arguably what is really needed is some form of comprehensive insurance entitling all injured persons to compensation from a central fund. Drug-induced injuries, like most accidents in a modern industrial society, may be viewed as part of the price of technological advance, and medicine benefits the public at large. A social security or state insurance model of risk allocation might seem more appropriate.

Such a scheme has recently been introduced in New Zealand. Under the Accidents Compensation Act 1972[40] (as amended) the common law negligence action has been abolished and replaced by an administrative system under which all accident victims, regardless of time, place or cause, are entitled to earnings-related compensation by way of periodical payments of 80 per cent of the loss (up to a maximum of about £120 a week). Only cases of wilful self-injury are excluded. The scheme is run by a State Accident Compensation Commission, which can employ insurance companies as agents. In place of third party liability insurance there is a government fund, financed from three main sources: levies on employers, on the self-employed and for motor vehicles. There is also a minor contribution from general taxation. The scheme is mainly concerned with loss of income, and lump sum awards for non-pecuniary loss are relatively small, with a maximum of about £9,500.

A solution of this kind naturally raises fundamental social and political issues, in addition to the difficulties of assessing its economic and administrative viability in societies more populous and industrialised than New Zealand. We do not start with a blank sheet. As Atiyah has demonstrated in his influential work, *Accidents, Compensation and the Law*, a root defect of our law on compensation is the lack of consistency as between the various systems which each operate according to their own criteria and interact in different ways with each other. In our mixed economy, private accident insurance, tort damages and welfare state benefits coexist.

Certainly there is a strong case for a more comprehensive approach. But the crucial question posed by solutions of the New Zealand variety is just how comprehensive can or ought they to be? Official estimates for mid-1974[41] indicated that there were in Great Britain 170,000 very

143

severely handicapped people, 380,000 severely handicapped and 660,000 appreciably handicapped, as well as another 350,000 people in hospitals and similar institutions. Those relying on welfare state provision far exceed in number the recipients of tort damages for personal injuries. Once the fault rationale has been abandoned, is there any justification, financial constraints apart, for singling out *accident* victims from the victims of disease or congenital disability for preferential treatment?[42] Why should the victim of a government-sponsored vaccination scheme be left financially worse off than the man who has contributed to his own injuries by careless driving? A child disabled after vaccination is not entitled to any special compensation. A complaint contesting this denial of redress has recently been brought before the European Commission of Human Rights by Mrs Rosemary Fox, secretary of the Association of Parents of Vaccine-Damaged Children, on behalf of 281 children believed to have been damaged by vaccination.[43] Several countries do provide compensation in these circumstances.[44] According to Mrs Fox, the government has not sufficiently explained the risks, in particular of whooping cough vaccine, for fear of endangering the national immunisation programme.

Similarly the late Richard Crossman observed in an article on disabled children:

> By the accident that a wealthy company could be held responsible [sic] for their misfortune, they [the thalidomide children] will become a tiny plutocratic élite while 8,500 children (many of them with disabilities just as grave as theirs) are condemned to lifelong incarceration in obsolete long-stay hospitals.[45]

Misgivings similar to those of Richard Crossman were voiced about the Congenital Disabilities (Civil Liability) Act 1976, when it was passing through Parliament. Based on a Law Commission Draft Bill,[46] its purpose is strictly limited. It seeks to clarify the legal position of children born disabled, first by providing *them* with a right of action where either parent is affected by a pre-natal occurrence which would normally have attracted tort liability. Here the child's remedy is derivative, arising if the parent is intentionally or negligently injured. Secondly, a father who is at fault would himself be liable to the child, though the mother would not (except in the case of negligent driving). The liability arises only on birth, so that no legal rights are given to the foetus and the abortion issue is not affected.

These proposals prompted a letter to *The Times*[47] from Lord Pearson, which we reproduce below, as it brings out well the inadequacies of the negligence approach and reservations about piecemeal legislation, while affording an insight into the lines along which the Commission is thinking:

Sir, The Congenital Disabilities (Civil Liability) Bill, which was introduced by Mr Ray Carter, MP, on December 17 last, is due to have its second reading in the House of Commons on February 6.

As the terms of reference of this Royal Commission include compensation for ante-natal injury, I think it right to state that my colleagues and I have misgivings about the Bill, which we have made clear to ministers.

It appears from paragraphs 2–6 of the Law Commission report, on which the Bill is based, that the Law Commission did not intend to prejudice the much wider issues of social policy with which the Royal Commission's report will be concerned, but only to establish the action of tort as applicable to ante-natal injuries in the meantime. It is important that this limitation should be accepted and recognized in Parliament.

Parliament should also be made aware of the special objections which can be and have been urged against relying on the operation of the tort action in the field of ante-natal injuries:

i   According to the expert evidence which we have received it is only in the rarest of cases that even the physical cause of a congenital deformity can be ascertained, and even if that is ascertainable the plaintiff in an action of tort would still have to prove that the deformity was caused by fault, usually negligence, on the part of the defendant.

ii   Thus the Bill, so far from dealing comprehensively with a widespread and highly distressing social problem, could result in compensation for no more than a minute proportion of the children concerned. The Bill, therefore, would raise many false hopes, not least by its very title.

iii   There would still be delay and expense, especially in difficult and complicated actions.

iv   The accusations and counter-accusations in such cases could have an adverse effect on family relations and on relations between doctors and patients. For example, in an action against a drug company or a doctor, the defence might allege that the damage to the unborn child was caused by the mother's own action such as smoking or drug addiction.

I hope it will be accepted that this Bill falls far short of providing a comprehensive solution to these problems. If it is passed, it will come into effect probably less than a year before the Royal Commission's report is presented, and that report may recommend a different system of compensation.

The Royal Commission understand why this Bill is being introduced but feel it right to draw attention to the complexities of the problem.

Yours faithfully,

PEARSON, Chairman,

Royal Commission on Civil Liability and Compensation for Personal Injury.

Yet despite the undoubted force behind these arguments, we feel that the Act is in principle justifiable as an interim measure. By eliminating residual doubts about the *right* to sue it will facilitate settlements in the admittedly small number of cases where it applies. Its detractors may be over-sanguine about the precise form the Pearson Commission's recommendations will take, not to mention the uncertainty as to when or whether they will be implemented.

Naturally no system will be without some anomalies, though an administrative scheme could avoid some of the indefensible procedural delays of a court-based system. At the same time it is worthy of note that New Zealand has thought fit to erect a complex review structure, including a dual right of appeal to the courts, to prevent abuse of the wide discretionary powers conferred on the administrative tribunal. Not for nothing, it seems, has the Accidents Compensation Act been dubbed the 'Lawyers' Compensation Act'!

Conclusion

Undoubtedly schemes of this kind are among the proposals before the Pearson Commission. But in the current economic climate the only prediction that can be made with safety is that no change involving major expenditure and disruption of existing institutions would be implemented for several years, even if approved in principle after exhaustive analysis of the financial implications. Road accidents and industrial injuries, which comprise the majority of negligence actions, and for which it would be easiest to build on the existing insurance framework, should be dealt with first if an order of priorities is required.

If one assumes that for defective products, strict liability within the tort system is the preferred alternative to negligence for the time being, we would argue that a piecemeal approach to it *is* desirable. It should be

146

apparent by now that there can be no all-purpose formula for products liability. The particular form it takes in any given industry needs to be worked out on the basis of as thorough a study as is practicable of the peculiarities of its market structure. In some respects this might point to taking a more lenient view of manufacturer responsibility for pharmaceuticals than for industry in general, given development risks, the high cost of research and development, the benefits to the public of drug innovation, and the number of cases where injury is not due to a defect in the drug.

On the other hand, probably no industry is better placed financially to bear the losses and, given the relative lack of competition, to distribute them. This last is the overriding consideration. The fears that stricter liability would stifle progress and severely damage the industry have not been borne out by the American experience. There are several plausible alternatives to the often ineffective negligence action. We would favour a form of products liability which is stricter than in practice obtains in the United States, namely strict liability, backed by insurance, for all defects where an effective available substitute would not have caused the injury.

Available financial data suggests that the industry is capable of bearing the increased burden this would entail in the ordinary course of events. To provide for catastrophic losses it might be possible to introduce compulsory insurance up to a given amount as a prerequisite of the right to market a drug, with the Government underwriting any excess. This would accord with the view that it bears a measure of responsibility by virtue of its role as a licensing agency, even if it is hardly realistic to expect governmental regulations and control to do much more than set minimum standards.

A further possibility would be to adopt a solution along the lines of the West German compensation fund financed by the pharmaceutical industry. The weakness of that particular scheme is that, being contingent on failure to prove fault against the defendant manufacturer, it seems to retain some of the procedural defects of the negligence action. Whatever system is adopted, the crucial element is that there should be some fund to which the plaintiff may have recourse without being wholly dependent on the capricious nature of the negligence action, or the vagaries of public campaigns.

To dwell exclusively on the horrors of the thalidomide tragedy and its aftermath would be to create a distorted picture of subsequent events. In concrete terms we have had the tightening up of controls and the introduction of new safety procedures under the Medicines Act. The rights of the unborn child to sue have been clarified in the Congenital Disabilities (Civil Liability) Act. Thalidomide was the catalyst for setting up the Pearson Commission on compensation and a major influence on the Phillimore Committee on Contempt. As often happens with changes in the law, the very enormity of the disaster and manifest inadequacy of the legal structure to cope may yet prove to be the spur to constructive reform.

Notes

[1] A comprehensive account is to be found in P.S. Atiyah's penetrating study, *Accidents, Compensation and the Law*, Weidenfeld and Nicolson (2nd ed.), 1975.

[2] For a brief résumé of these schemes, see B.A. Hepple and M.H. Matthews, *Tort: Cases and Materials*, Butterworths 1974, Appendix G.

[3] *Nettleship* v. *Weston* [1971] 2 Q.B.691.

[4] *Canadian Bar Review*, vol.51, 1973, p.155.

[5] Ibid., p.157.

[6] Ibid., p.159.

[7] T.G. Ison, *The Forensic Lottery*, Staples Press 1967.

[8] See Atiyah, *Accidents, Compensation and the Law*, ch.21.

[9] The American literature is voluminous. See in particular W.L. Prosser, 'The Assault upon the Citadel', *Yale Law Journal*, vol.69, 1960, p.1099 and 'The Fall of the Citadel', *Minnesota Law Review*, vol.50, 1966, p.791.

[10] S.4(7). See also Fair Trading Act 1973, s.137(2).

[11] See, e.g., Uniform Commercial Code, s.2–318.

[12] For example, *Perlmutter* v. *Beth David Hospital* (1954), 123 N.E. 2d 792, where liability was denied. But see now *Cunningham* v. *MacNeal Memorial Hospital* (1970), 47 Ill. 2d 443.

[13] See *Greenman* v. *Yuba Power Products Inc.* (1962), 377 P.2d 897.

[14] As in *Escola* v. *Coca Cola Bottling Co.* (1944), 24 C.2d 453, *per* Traynor J.

[15] See H. Teff, 'Products Liability in the Pharmaceutical Industry at Common Law', *McGill Law Journal*, vol.20, 1974, p.102.

[16] (1966), 409 P.2d 904.

[17] Comment k.

[18] Ibid.

[19] (1971), 15 Cal. App. 3d 75.

[20] Ibid., p.79.

[21] P. Keeton, 'Manufacturer's Liability: The Meaning of "Defect" in the Manufacture and Design of Products', *Syracuse Law Review*, vol.20, 1969, p.559, at 571.

[22] For example, C.H. Kubey, 'Strict Liability in Tort: Its Applicability to Manufacturers of Prescription Drugs', *University of California Davis Law Review*, vol.7, 1974, p.487, at 505.

[23] A. Ehrenzweig, *Negligence Without Fault*, University of California 1951.

[24] See Keeton, op. cit., p.563.

[25] See Association Européenne d'Etudes Juridiques et Fiscales, *Product Liability in Europe*, Kluwer-Harrap 1975.

[26] BGH, NJW 69, 269 (*Fowl Pest* case).

[27] P. Prag, 'A Comparative Study of Products Liability', *Legal Issues of European Integration*, vol.1, 1975, p.109.

[28] Draft European Convention on Products Liability in regard to Personal Injury and Death.

[29] Art. 3(1), (2).

[30] Art. 5.

[31] DM30 million, or its equivalent, for all damage caused by identical products having the same defect. Draft Convention, Annex 2(b).

[32] DM500,000, or its equivalent, for each person injured or killed, and DM200 million for all damage caused by identical products having the same effect: 1974 draft *Arzneimittelgesetz* (Drug Registration and Administration Law) *Bundesrat*, Drucksache 552/74.

[33] Memorandum on the approximation of the laws of member states relating to product liability.

[34] *Product Liability in Europe*, p.21.

[35] Working Paper No. 64, HMSO 1975.

[36] Ibid., p.43.

[37] Ibid., pp.64 and 71.

[38] *Accidents, Compensation and the Law*, p.357.

[39] D.R. Harris, 'Accident Compensation in New Zealand: A Comprehensive Insurance System', *Modern Law Review*, vol.37, 1974, p.361.

[40] Accidents Compensation Act, No. 43 of 1972 (as amended in 1973).

[41] See Central Office of Information, *Care of Disabled People in Britain*, HMSO 1975, p.6.

[42] The more radical Australian National Compensation Bill 1974 (as

amended), which provided for compensation for significant physical or mental incapacity due to *any* cause, lapsed with the change of government at the end of 1975.

[43] The association claims that by promoting a regular immunisation scheme and failing to warn parents of the possible health risks involved, the Government are in breach of Art. 2 of the European Convention on Human Rights (right to life) and Art. 8 (right to respect for private and family life).

[44] For example, Germany: Bundesseuchengesetz, 18 July 1961, (1961) 1 BGBL 1012.

[45] *The Times* 18 July 1973.

[46] See The Law Commission, *Report on Injuries to Unborn Children*, HMSO 1974, Cmnd. 5709, Appendix I.

[47] *The Times* 28 January 1976.

Author index

Subject index

Regulation of pharmaceuticals: in United
Kingdom 111−18, 124−5; in United
States 118−25
Research, pharmaceutical 104−6, 147
Richardson-Merrell Inc. 5, 7, 34, 107,
132
Royal Commission on Civil Liability *see*
Pearson Commission

Safety of drugs 107−12, 114−17,
135−8, 148
Sainsbury Committee 105, 115
Sale of goods, law of 43−6
Satherley, Mr and Mrs 11
Schmidt, Alexander 125
Scott, Sir Ronald Bodley 116
Scowen, Sir Eric 112, 116, 118
Senate Sub-committee on Antitrust and
Monopoly 121−2
Settlement: abroad 14, 19; the early
10−13, 27, 48, 58; the final 18−25;
the settlement process 57−61
Side effects *see* Safety of drugs
Sinclair, Upton 119
Society for the Aid of Thalidomide
Children 10

Sunday Times 10, 13, 16, 19, 21−5, 30,
36, ch.3 *passim*, 129

Taussig, Dr H. 5, 120
Teratogenicity *see* Foetal deformity
Testing of thalidomide 2, 30−40, 68
Thomson, Lord 66, 97
Times, The 10
Triparanol *see* Mer/29
Trades Union Congress 18

Unborn child 12, 19, 27, 40−2, 129,
144−6
United States 4, 5, 7, 14, 15, 19, 34,
39−41, 50, 96−7, 106−8, 111,
118−25, 127, 132−8, 141, 147

Vaccines 108, 144
Valium 104, 105, 110
Voluntary Price Regulation Schemes 104

Washington Post 96, 122
Watergate 96−7
Wiley, H.W. 118
Wilson, Professor Graham 9
Wilson, Harold 96, 103
World Health Organisation 103, 111

The authors

Harvey Teff graduated in law from Oxford University and holds an LL.M. and a PhD from London University. He was called to the Bar in 1965. He has lectured in law at Durham University since 1969, becoming Senior Lecturer in 1975.

Colin Munro is a graduate in law of the University of Aberdeen. He lectured at the University of Birmingham and has held his present post as Lecturer in Law at the University of Durham since 1972.